Prophets of Revolution

Prophets of Revolution

Peter Asael Gonzalez
with Dan Wooding

Foreword by Brother Andrew

HODDER AND STOUGHTON
LONDON · SYDNEY · AUCKLAND · TORONTO

All Scripture quotations are taken from the Revised Standard Version.

British Library Cataloguing in Publication Data

Gonzales, Peter Asael
  Prophets of revolution
  i. Latin American – Politics Government – 1948
  ii. Christianity politics
  I. Title   II. Wooding, Dan
  261.7   BR115

ISBN 0 340 32372 8

Hodder and Stoughton Editorial Office: 47 Bedford Square, London WC1B 3DP

Mexican-born Peter Asael Gonzalez is the eldest son in a remarkable family. Each of his brothers and sisters has responded in a different way to the revolutionary climate of the times in their explosive region of the world. All these 'prophets of revolution' have a burning Christian faith that has led them to get deeply involved in Latin American affairs.

Dan Wooding is a British journalist and writer who travelled all over Latin America with Peter Asael Gonzalez in researching this book, his fifteenth. He was chief reporter with *The Christian* in London, and later a senior reporter with both the *Sunday People* and the *Sunday Mirror*. He is married to Norma, and they have two sons, Andrew and Peter.

Some names and locations in this book have been changed for the protection of those featured in these pages.

Contents

Dedication

To my father, Cesar, an example of someone who has courageously fought against adversity.

To my mother, Olivia, who guided me into membership of a very special 'royal family' – the family of God.

To my beloved wife, Blanca, who has been the strongest support to me during the many ups and downs of my ministry to Latin America.

To my four children, Nellie, Azael, Eduardo and Ali, for whom I pray each night that they will always behave with the dignity that befits a member of a 'royal family'.

To my brothers and sisters whom I greatly admire and respect for their dedication to serve the suffering people of Latin America.

And finally, I wish to dedicate this book to all the people of Latin America. I hope that one day we will all be united and be able to lift up our hands in welcome to our returning Lord Jesus Christ.

Peter Asael Gonzalez

Foreword

This book, *Prophets of Revolution*, tells a true story . . .
one all too characteristic of Latin America today. It
recounts, through the eyes of my very good friend, Peter
Asael Gonzalez, the dilemma Latin American youth faces
in building their lives and having to choose between
competing political systems.

I've watched this tug-of-war take place in many lives.
I've witnessed the consequences.

It was early morning in Costa Rica and I was in the coffee
shop of my hotel. Just across the table a mother sat and
shared her story. Her heartbreak was the heartbreak of
millions of fathers and mothers who have come up against a
new world system . . . and lost the first round.

In this case, a mother had lost her daughter. The plea of
her heart was, 'How can I get my daughter back?'

'Recruiters came to this country with promises,
promises; and my daughter and many others with her, all
promising young people of this country, received an offer
they had never received before – free academic studies.
The future would be theirs, once they returned.'

But what was not said was how they would return, nor
even if they would return.

The mother, tears in her eyes, told me that her daughter
was now in a city in Siberia, a place I knew well.

I'd preached in that city, although such was not allowed.
I had not seen any foreign students in the services. I knew
full well they would not be allowed to go to church.

Even if they had insisted, 'I want to go home!' there

would be no way to go home. They were trapped.

Today in Latin America not all the young people have to go as far away as Siberia or Eastern Europe. There's a place much closer by, where they can be taught in Spanish. Again, thousands of young people have been trapped.

All go on the same promise, 'Come, we will pay for your study; we'll make you a leader.'

But what they fail to say is, 'We will make you a revolutionary leader, a terrorist leader.'

What they fail to say is that there is little religious liberty. If the young people still have any convictions, they will be stamped out in the course of their studies.

This is the battle that we face. Sad to say, many thousands of parents and young people have lost that first round.

I remember once I met an African student in a city in Eastern Europe. Strangely enough, I met him in church. He had the guts to go to church!

Afterwards he sought me out to tell me his sorry tale. This very same thing had happened to him. A man had come and called a group of bright young students together.

'What do you want to be? What do you want your country to be? What role do you want to play? Won't you come to our country and study? We offer you free academic studies – we'll even pay for your trip, give you pocket money, pay all your expenses. You'll get a thorough education, then you can come home and become a leader in your country. Any questions?'

Plenty of questions: 'Where? How?'

'Eastern Europe!'

'But that's a communist area. There's no religious liberty. We have all had our education in mission schools. We can't go to an atheist country to study. Whatever future you promise, how about liberty of religion? Can we serve God? Can we go to church?'

With a smile, the reassuring answer came: 'There's no persecution in our country. As a matter of fact, we're all Christians. Let's close this meeting in prayer.'

Then the recruiter had them bow their heads. He had the

audacity to pray with them, to prove with his actions that indeed they would go to a Christian country.

'Let's go back to the village and talk it over with our parents, with our pastor.'

'Oh, no,' he said. 'It happens that the plane leaves tomorrow morning. There's no way you can go home!'

That's how this young fellow got to Eastern Europe. Trapped, he couldn't get out. He couldn't even go to church . . . unless he accepted the punishment of low grades, and the possibility of never graduating.

He had no way to go home because his way would have to be paid in hard currency, and how does any student, particularly one from a developing country, get dollars in a communist country? No way back!

That was only one of the experiences that flooded my thoughts as I looked at this mother in Costa Rica.

In this book you will read a dramatic story of the young people of just one Latin America family. The Gonzalez family are real people and although their names are changed, every story is real. Peter is a dynamic Christian leader who faithfully follows His Lord.

Just as the Gonzalez children had to make their decisions, so countless Latin American young people have to respond to the revolutionary realities of the countries that we are concerned with.

Are we really losing a battle, or is there a way out? Do we have a message? Is there a way to reach these young people of Latin America?

What is the alternative?

Whom do we blame when the Communists are successful? Can we blame the young people from Latin America, Africa, and Asia for accepting the most fantastic offer they've ever received?

We, as Christians, have never offered them so much. We perhaps have never offered them the future, or even the dignity which is being shown them from the other side.

We are losing round after round in this battle. But it's not too late!

That same day in Costa Rica as I picked up my Bible for

my daily reading, I saw a verse which came to me as a strong message from the Lord. It is John 9:4; 'Night comes, when no one can work.'

As I looked around me in Latin America, I saw dark clouds on every side. Night *is* coming! God spoke to me so clearly.

Later that morning, I shared the message with a group of theologians and pastors. Somehow I had the feeling that the message was received until we attended a lunch with a number of the same pastors and theologians.

One of the leading theologians came to me and said, 'Andrew, we've looked it up in the original. John 9:4 probably only refers to the following night when Jesus was going to be arrested. On that night they would not be able to do any work. It has no further meaning to us today.'

My heart sank. Again the words rang in my ears, 'Night comes, when no one can work' not the church in Latin America, not even Open Doors. No more work!

I pray that as you read this book, your eyes will be opened. But that means that we will have to accept responsibility for these young people. We must be ready to train and encourage them as they take their place of Christian leadership to become true prophets of a revolution of love, in their nations and for their continent.

This will also be our salvation.

Here is the battlefield for the hearts and minds of young people who face an uncertain future. If we don't make a firm offer to lead them, support them, and train them, then the other side surely will do so. When they do, don't blame them for doing it.

Unfriendly political systems, just as untaught religious sects, are the unpaid bills of the church. It's time we pay . . . now or later. . . .

Brother Andrew

Acknowledgments

It may seem strange that a Mexican and an Englishman should be brought together for a project such as this. Yet the two of us, from such differing cultures, became one in the writing of this book.

As we travelled together all over Latin America, meeting my family and soaking up the many customs and traditions of the continent, an unbreakable bond was established between us.

I would like to thank Dan Wooding for his tireless work on this book, and pray that the story we are about to share with you will challenge and inspire you not only to comprehend the problems of my tortured land, but also to see some of the spiritual solutions to those problems.

I would like also to place on record my gratitude to Brother Andrew for the inspiration he has been to me and also for bringing to my life a new dimension of service to those members of the Body of Christ who suffer in silence. He helped me to see that with the power of Jesus Christ, they can be, in that suffering, more than conquerors.

I also thank my dear friend, Dr. Dale W. Kietzman, a leader in Open Doors and the one who brought me into this ministry, for suggesting this book and for his constant encouragement to me.

I would especially like to express my appreciation to the Latin America team of Open Doors who helped me so much with the transcription and translation of tapes and their typing of the manuscript, and also to Dan Wooding's son Andrew, who spent many hours typing up various drafts of the book in England.

I also wish to give thanks to the staff and students of the Biblical Seminary at Puebla, Mexico, for it was there that I was guided in my first faltering steps of faith in the Christian life;

to the Latin American Mission, for introducing me to evangelistic service in the continent;

to the various Bible societies in Latin America, for teaching me how to use the Word of God as a manual for liberation and hope for the human being, and then showing me how to teach others these skills;

to Hermano Pablo and those involved in his radio and television ministry for opening my eyes to a massive and dynamic form of evangelism through mass media communication;

to the 'John 17:21 International' movement, for filling my heart with the necessity of the unity of the Body of Christ 'so that the world might believe'.

And finally, I thank the world-wide family of Open Doors with Brother Andrew International for their deep fellowship and love.

To all of you, '*Muchas Gracias*'.

Peter Asael Gonzalez

1. Explosions in my Head

There was a sudden blinding barrage of rocket shells, quickly followed by the chatter of machine-gun fire. A cloud of billowing black smoke rose to obscure the lovely violet of dusk.

'Quick, close the curtains; switch off the lights and get under the bed,' I yelled to Shaun, my Irish companion. 'I think the hotel's being attacked by the Sandinistas.'

My heart was thudding heavily and my legs felt like water as I eased myself under the bed. My back soon began to hurt as I lay prostrate on the rough concrete floor. I wanted to swallow, but my mouth was too dry.

Shaun, a suave businessman in his late forties, had lived in Nicaragua for about two years. He whispered quietly from under his bed, 'Peter, this is the closest they've ever been.'

Another blast shook the room, and the timbers began to creak. The air by now was acrid with the smell of death and destruction.

I was in Nicaragua in June 1979. The government of Anastasio Somoza was in its death throes. Somoza and his family had ruled with an iron fist over Nicaraguan affairs for some forty-five years, and his father and brother had preceded Anastasio Somoza as president. The dynasty had enriched itself to the extent of hundreds of millions of dollars, secured ownership of over a quarter of the cultivatable land, and came to own the national airline and steamship company, plus eighty-five other industrial establishments.

The revolt had been initiated by the *Frente Sandinista de Liberacion Nacional* (Sandinista Front of National Liberation) – F.S.L.N. – named after a Nicaraguan national hero, Augusto Cesar Sandino, 1895–1934. F.S.L.N. began as a small guerrilla force in 1961. The assassination by Somoza guards of Pedro Joaquin Chamorro, the courageous anti-Somoza editor of the conservative *La Prensa*, on January 10th, 1978, brought almost all sectors of the Nicaraguan population to the side of the revolution.

At the time of my visit, the Sandinistas, a loose coalition of Marxists and non-Marxist Social Democrats, were pressing home their advantage against Somoza's storm troopers, the National Guard. Even as I was driven in from the airport, I had seen the results of their attacks: tumbled walls, burned and fallen roofs, torn-up streets, tangled and shredded telephone and electrical wires. Roadblocks had been erected by F.S.L.N. supporters, who had pulled up thousands of *adoquinas* (pavement bricks) in their fierce determination to defend their neighbourhood against Somoza's bloody National Guard.

It was easy to be sympathetic with the Nicaraguan people in their struggle. But whatever I had thought about the revolution, I knew now that I could soon become a mangled victim of it. The thought forced my nerves to crank up another notch. Everything now blurred around that one pre-occupation: staying alive.

I recalled Lenin's phrase, 'The purpose of terror is to terrify.' It was certainly true in this case. The frightening sound of exploding bombs cut into the heavy air.

'All we can do, Peter, is to pray, and ask the Lord to protect us,' Shaun said in a calm, untroubled voice. I'd met him at the airport and accepted his kind offer to share his room. He'd seen that I had nowhere to stay. Although he was still a new Christian, on that incredibly long night Shaun showed me how quickly he had advanced as a believer. An unusual under-the-beds prayer meeting was soon in progress in our room.

'Lord,' I prayed, cotton-mouthed with fear, 'We are in

your hands. If it is your will, I'm ready to die, but if it isn't, and if you don't mind, I'd rather stay alive.'

With that, Shaun gave a thin and nervous chuckle. I prayed on, my voice almost inaudible above the mayhem going on around the hotel, located on the edge of the capital city of Managua. Thoughts of my family drifted into my mind. The image of my wife's face was clearly in front of me, outlined in the darkness in every detail. Her deep hazel eyes, her ebony hair.

'What's going to happen to her, or my four children, if I die, Lord? Who will take care of them?'

I had been in many dangerous situations during my travels throughout Latin America but fear gripped me especially tightly that night.

'Peter, can you hear me from under there?'

'Yes, Shaun. What is it?' I whispered hoarsely.

'Look, my friend, during my brief time as a Christian living through the troubles here, I have learned by heart a verse which has really helped me.'

'What is it?'

'It's Matthew 10:28, and reads: ". . . do not fear those who kill the body but cannot kill the soul; rather fear him who can destroy both soul and body in hell".'

Shaun paused for a moment to allow those powerful words to sink in, then continued:

'Another verse I can recall is Psalm 116:15, "Precious in the sight of the Lord is the death of his saints".'

His voice was edged with steel now.

'Peter, if we die we will go to be with Him. That, surely, is not that terrible, is it?'

I reluctantly muttered my agreement. I was astonished and not a little shamefaced that here was a 'baby Christian' giving me mature advice. After all, I had been a Christian for twenty years and it should have been the other way around!

'Shaun,' I conceded, 'you have taught me a great lesson today. Those of us who have known the Lord for a long time often feel we know everything. We have studied theology, but I think sometimes we forget that the Bible

21

verses we learned have a practical application. Often they become just head knowledge to us instead of God's Living Word.'

I thanked Shaun and then began to share with him details of my many treks across Latin America.

'You know, Shaun, this area of the world used to be so happy-go-lucky. People had smiles. Now all I hear is gunfire. It's hard to understand what is going on. There are so many troubles all over the region.'

As I spoke, I recognised that still small voice which I knew was the Lord's, telling me to get hold of a Bible and turn to Exodus 3:7. I slipped cautiously out from under the far from secure cover of my bed and grabbed my Bible. I also picked up a small torch which I had brought with me.

In a light as thin as buttermilk, I screwed up my eyes to read: 'And the Lord said, "I have seen the affliction of my people who are in Egypt, and have heard their cry because of their taskmasters; I know their sufferings." ' Then in verse 8: 'I have come down to deliver them out of the hand of the Egyptians, and bring them up out of that land to a good and broad land flowing with milk and honey . . .'

I began to question aloud whether the Sandinistas guerrillas were, in fact, the answer from God to the anguished cry of the Nicaraguan people.

'The Nicaraguans have suffered more than we can tell,' I said to Shaun. 'I've been told that at least fifty per cent of those over ten years of age here cannot read and write.'

'That's terrible,' the Irishman responded in his soft, lilting voice.

'Then they had the earthquake in 1972 which just about wiped out Managua and killed thousands. My friend, with troubles like that, they could do without a man like Somoza who has been bleeding them dry.'

Shaun agreed, and hoped that our room was not bugged and that none of Somoza's men were listening in to our conversation.

'Latin people do smile a lot,' I went on. 'But maybe those smiles I have seen were just a mask; maybe the people didn't really want to show their real pain.'

As I lay on that rock-hard hotel floor, mosquitos began probing my arm, then a cockroach scuttled by. I twisted my head to relieve a crick in my neck.

Shaun eventually dozed off and I let my mind wander. Soon I began to mouth silent questions.

'Lord, what am I doing here? What are you trying to teach me? None of this makes sense.'

I had come to the country representing a Christian television network. I was to set up a series of meetings for pastors, following the principle of John 17:21, which says, '. . . that they may all be one; even as thou, Father, art in me, and I in thee, that they also may be in us, so that the world may believe that thou hast sent me.'

These were to be meetings that brought together Christian leaders to work as 'one'. I had quickly realised, however, that in Nicaragua some of the older pastors felt that, since Somoza did allow freedom of religion, they were obliged to be subservient to the government in power. Others believed that Somoza was administering injustice instead of justice, and that they had the right to revolution.

Many Christian young people had joined the guerrillas. Some church buildings had suffered from the aerial bombings by the National Guard, and the Sandinistas sometimes used church buildings as their general head-quarters when they took over towns.

On this trip much of my head-learning was shaken. For instance, I couldn't understand why the Church in Nicaragua was so divided. Instead of being a strong force for good, many of the denominations were fighting each other.

'Could it be, Lord, that the Sandinistas are actually being used by you to help the people?' This question nagged. I could see how the common people in Nicaragua had been exploited, but surely violence couldn't be right. Or could it?

'God, if you are behind the revolution, why not help the Sandinistas in their fighting?'

Even as I prayed, I felt chills run down my spine. I did not know whether or not I should have asked the Lord to help these men who were so violently trying to rid the country of a dictator.

'Life is so much more simple for a Christian in Mexico,' I observed under my breath. 'We have a more stable society. Maybe you are making me face up to the harsh realities of life in an unfair society. You are making me see that my faith has to be real, not just theory.' I lay back and closed my eyes, hoping rest would come. Gradually I lapsed into a fitful sleep.

I awoke with a start as sunlight streamed into the room. The battle had ended, for a few hours at least. The city was coming to life again, with cars noisily passing by outside the hotel. Was last night just a bad dream?

'Shaun, could you take me to the airport? I think I'll try to get a flight out today.' I couldn't get out of the war zone quickly enough.

At the international terminal on the edge of Managua, I eventually managed to get a flight to Costa Rica. As we took off and zoomed skyward, I gave thanks to the Lord.

'This is like a resurrection, Lord. Thank you so much that I am still alive.'

As I looked down at the lush green landscape of that terror-torn land, I realised that the Sandinistas had taught me a big lesson. They were a *united front*! They were serving each other as one for a common cause.

'Lord, this is something that the Church in Latin America is not doing. They are not working together. They are not a serving Church the way they should be. Please help me to be a servant of my people in this hemisphere. I need revolutionary ideas from you which will bring them together and give them true freedom.'

2. A Royal Family

My mother peered at me over the bridge of her nose. Her face, as always, was pale as porcelain. She fixed me with a reproachful eye.

'Peter, why did you use that bad word?'

'I picked it up at school, Mama. Everyone speaks like that there.'

'My son,' she paused to add emphasis to her words. 'You should not want to be like the rest of the people. You have to look higher than that.'

I felt her sharp pinch on my arm. Mother always did that to us when she was really upset. 'Peter, I want you to become a good Christian. I want you to be different.'

I was just five years old and we were living in a working-class *barrio* (community) in Victoria City, located in the northern region of Mexico. Papa would often be away for days, driving a bus for his father's bus company, and so we didn't see much of him. Consequently, Mother became responsible for most of the discipline in our home.

I was surprised that my father never had a traffic accident as he had sight only in his left eye. He lost his right eye at the age of six. I discovered later in life that he had suffered from glaucoma, a disease of the eye marked by increased pressure within the eye's optic disc, causing a gradual loss of vision.

One day he set me on his knee and pointed to the shadowed hollow where his eye had been. Then he told me the disturbing story.

'It was the eye specialist's fault.' My father's voice was

25

without rancour. 'He kept telling me that nothing was wrong with my eye and that it would get better. He gave me drops and told me to keep putting them in my damaged eye. But it got worse and worse and eventually, after a year, the pain was so bad that I went to another doctor. He had no alternative but to take out my eye.

'The doctor wanted to give me a glass replacement, but I wouldn't take it. I didn't want to pretend that I could see through it when I couldn't. "I am what I am," I told the doctor. "If that is to be my life, I am ready to fight for it." '

My father smiled. His good eye gleamed. 'Take this as an example, son. Be what you are. Don't follow the crowd.'

In order to support our growing family which eventually comprised four boys and four girls, he would also buy and sell almost anything – chickens, oranges, whatever he could make a profit on.

Soon I realised that if I wanted any little extras in my life, I had to go out into the street and try to earn some money for myself. Like millions of other families in my country, we only just had enough to eat.

When I was six years old, I began selling lettuce and cabbage around the streets of a *barrio* one mile from ours. I would leave home in the dark at five a.m. to collect the green vegetables from my friend Tito's backyard. Tito had told me, 'Peter, if you take this cabbage and lettuce out into the streets of the posh *barrio* and sell them before school, my papa will pay you eighteen cents.' That was a fortune to me. With such an amount I could buy a small soda pop and a cookie. What a prospect!

I remember my first selling trip into the strange new land outside my *barrio*. Those two blocks surrounding us were all that we knew about life. At the back of our home was a river and that marked the border of our territory. We never dared venture across the bridge that spanned it because we knew it would take us into a new world. That was too frightening for words.

However, Flash Gordon changed all that! One day at the local cinema, I saw this superhuman hero invading the planet 'Mongo'. I decided then, at once, that I was going to be as daring as he. Well, not quite, but I would at least try to 'invade' the next *barrio*.

After stocking up with my cargo of cabbages and lettuce, I began my daring foray. I gasped in amazement as I suddenly saw that this world had street lamps. We had none. It also had pavement stones. Large, impressive houses rose up from behind wrought-iron fences.

I decided to try to sell my wares at a huge white house that caught my eye. It was surrounded by a neatly manicured lawn. I knocked at the gate with a stone. (I was then so small that I couldn't reach the bell!) Suddenly a huge boxer dog, drooling and baring its teeth, rose up at the gate and began to snarl menacingly at me. My heart bumped against the walls of my tiny chest, and I ran terrified up the road. After about two hundred yards, I panted to a halt and sat down on a wall. There was sweat between my knuckles. It was then that I felt ashamed.

'What would Flash have done?' I thought. 'Surely he wouldn't have run away like a scared baby.'

Right, that was it! I was going back to conquer that snarling beast and get my sale. I tiptoed to the house, but the ferocious growling made me back off again. It wasn't going to be easy to be a hero.

So I just stared straight into the dog's eyes. He sat transfixed for some fifteen minutes as I stared him out almost unblinkingly.

I was in a trance-like state when, suddenly, the woman of the house came out and shooed the dog away. It scooted across the lawn and I jumped with surprise as she addressed me.

'Boy, you are very brave. I've been watching you from the window. I think you deserve my trade.' The lady was obviously very rich. Her fingers sparkled with jewellery.

'I'll take one cabbage and one lettuce.'

'Thank you, ma'am.'

What a moment! I lovingly fingered the thirty cents she gave me. Flash would have been proud of me.

When I got to our *barrio*, I recounted the story to my friends. A crowd gathered outside the Fixed Price Store, where much of our life centred. It was a little wooden open-fronted shop which sold everything from food to brooms. Its name stemmed from the fact that no haggling was allowed.

'You know, I actually risked my life,' I told my friends as their eyes widened. 'It was like visiting another planet. Just like Flash Gordon.'

'Can we come on your next adventure, Peter?' they chorused.

'Of course,' I said benevolently.

There and then, although I didn't realise it, I had broken through a *barrio* tradition. Up until that moment, the rich boys were the leaders, since they were the ones who could bribe their followers with free candy. But now a poor adventurer had taken their place. Where should I lead my 'men'? The answer came the next day at the nearby primary school I attended. I overheard a group of boys discussing the Indian cave, apparently once the home of an Indian, which was five blocks from us. To get to it entailed a trip across the river.

'Oh, yes,' I heard one seven-year-old boy say. 'I go in there all the time. I go with my friends. We take cigarettes and smoke; it's great. No one has ever found us there.'

That was it! I had to take my people to the cave. We would have a quick puff of a cigarette to prove our bravery, then return. That would certainly be an adventure. I discovered where the cave was located and called a gang meeting.

On the dirt road outside the Fixed Price Store I drew a map showing where this cave was. I then asked for suggestions for reaching this place without being followed.

'I think we should wade across the river in darkness and then go through the back streets,' said one boy.

'No, we could drown,' I countered. 'Let's just walk across the bridge.' That was agreed and I quickly destroyed the dust map with my feet.

Pepe, one of the rich kids, managed to get hold of a whole packet of cigarettes and the next evening, just as darkness was falling, we set off. We tiptoed the whole way through the darkened, rough streets, hearing the sounds from within houses of children crying and of housewives slapping tortillas into shape. An occasional lone pedlar cried his wares, and a drunken man staggered by me uttering curses to himself. With the help of my torch, we finally found the little cave.

'O.K., Pepe, the cigarettes and matches.' I, as leader, had to take the first 'drag'.

I had never before tasted a cigarette, and I began choking as the harsh smoke hit my lungs. I almost lost my dare-devil gang there and then, but I quickly recovered my composure and handed the noxious weed to the next in line. All too soon the excitement was over and we began shivering with the evening cold, so we headed back to our *barrio*, and reality as we knew it.

Besides leading my little platoon on several more adventures, I continued to sell cabbages and lettuce around the wealthy area. Eventually, however, I thought there was possibly a better way of earning a living. I had watched shoe-shine boys at work locally and they seemed to be doing quite well for themselves. So I decided to make my own shoe-shine box out of some wood I had discovered in my father's junk room.

My mother's eyes glowed with pleasure when she saw the result of my handicraft efforts.

'Here, son,' she said proudly, 'take these tins of polish and these new brushes and do a good job. You have my blessing.'

So, after a morning at school, I took my shoe-shine box into the streets to try to earn a few cents. Even if I wasn't earning a fortune, I was now making my way in the world. I had self-respect.

Then came my big break. When I was nine, my grandfather Emilio, a tall florid-faced man with blond hair (highly unusual in Mexico) and a powerful personality, sent a message for me to come to his bus company office. I shivered with anticipation at his door, wondering what terrible crime I had committed. He had a way of making one feel guilty for no reason.

'Peter, sit down,' he boomed, drumming his finger tips on the huge mahogany desk. 'Is it true that you do shoe-shines in the streets?'

He seemed to look straight into my heart.

'Yes, Grandpapa Emilio.'

'Well, I want you to come and work here. I want you to bring your box here every day after school and shine the shoes of all my visitors. You will become a businessman. You will keep all your profits.' There was a ghost of a smile on his face.

'Thank you, sir,' was all I could stammer out. 'I won't let you down.'

Soon I was making so much money from my shoe venture that I was able to invest in a custom-made box and even purchase new brushes. But although I was indeed now a businessman, I still didn't have a bicycle. The rich kids of the *barrio*, those whose parents ran stores, had bicycles. So that had to be my next project.

My father's junk room once again yielded up a prize. My eyes gleamed as I came across the dark red frame and rusting rims of an ancient bike. I took a stone and began trying to knock the twisted wheels into shape. I bought a little can of oil for the chain. But still it didn't have tyres.

For five months, I went hopefully to the local garbage dump, and at last two old tyres were thrown there. Excitedly, I borrowed a pump from a cycle owner and blew up the inner-tubes inside the tyres. But the air just rushed out. Both tubes were peppered with large holes. I tried instant repairs with sticking plaster, which at least temporarily stopped most of the air escaping. I patched the holes in the tyres themselves from the inside with cardboard.

Then came the moment of truth. I had to ride it. I took my new bicycle into the street and basked in the admiring glances of the others. I clambered aboard and wobbled along for a few yards, then I fell off. The ground crunched under my body.

'The wheels are not really round, so riding it is not easy,' I laughed nervously, giving explanations to the small crowd as I picked myself up and dusted myself down.

With a bow to my friends, I took the bicycle back into my home. It wasn't really important whether I could ride it properly or not. I had achieved what was important: to own a bicycle.

Mother made it clear, however, that there had to be another dimension in my life – a spiritual one.

'Peter,' she said to me one day, 'I want to show you a Bible verse.' She dragged down from a shelf our large family Bible and fluttered the pages until she came to 1 Peter 2:9. Then she read carefully, ' "But you are a chosen race, a royal priesthood, a holy nation, God's own people, that you may declare the wonderful deeds of Him who called you out of darkness into His marvellous light."

'You must always remember, Peter, that you are a royal person.'

Each Sunday, Mother would take me, along with my elder sister, Nellie, and my two younger brothers, Cesar and Ruben, to the local Presbyterian church. First we would attend Sunday School and then afterwards the morning service. It was an important part of our early upbringing.

The Bible always seemed to play a big part in Mother's life. I recall one day when Rosa, one of my sisters, came home from school and confessed that she had been in trouble for bad behaviour. Mother locked her in her bedroom with a Bible and ordered her to read it.

'It is very important that you read and understand the Scriptures so that you can change your bad behaviour,' she told Rosa.

Mother kept on reminding us that we were part of a royal family. We were different from the herd. The fact of that difference was brought home to me one day when I went to see Beto, my cousin, who lived half a block from our home. He was my age. When I walked through the back door his mother was making *chorizo* (Mexican sausage) to sell to friends in the area.

'Hey, Peter, do you want to see something?' Beto greeted me excitedly. He signalled me to follow him into

31

the back yard where he had a fishing rod already set up. It was baited on the hook with some of his mother's sausage.

'Don't make a sound,' he hissed.

Suddenly a tabby cat appeared and approached the *chorizo* and made a grab for it. Beto's face twisted unpleasantly and he began winding the rod at great speed. The cat screeched in pain as the hook tore inside its mouth.

'Beto!' My voice was hoarse, husky, unbelieving. 'Stop! That's cruel.'

Beto only laughed.

Eventually he unhooked the yelping, screaming cat. I thought he had at last seen sense. But then he grabbed a burlap sack and dropped the blood-soaked cat into it. He tied the top of the sack and roughly dropped it to the ground. I watched in horror as Beto grabbed the spear he used for fishing and brutally hurled it at the sack. The squealing continued for a brief moment and then all went quiet. The cat was dead. It was a vile act by Beto.

Tears of shock and anger coursed down my cheeks.

'You are very cruel,' I told my cousin.

He laughed aloud and punched the air in triumph.

'You're just soft, Peter. Those cats steal Mama's sausage. I'm protecting her investment.'

I looked at my cousin. 'God's going to judge you one day for that, Beto.' I knew that what he had done was wrong.

'Oh, that's a lot of baloney. You don't really believe all that religious stuff, do you?' His lips curled into a sneer.

That night in my bedroom I couldn't stop crying. The strangled sound of the dying cat kept coming into my mind. I was making such a noise that my mother came in to comfort me.

'Why, Mama, would Beto do such a thing? His family has lots of money. Yet he doesn't act like he belongs to a royal family.'

My mother sat beside my bed. She reached across and squeezed my hand. 'I am going to fetch the Bible and I will read a verse to you. Then you'll understand.'

'Peter,' she said as she returned, 'this is from Matthew, chapter 6, verses 19 to 21. It reads, "Do not lay up for yourselves treasures on earth, where moth and rust consume and where thieves break in and steal, but lay up for yourselves treasures in heaven, where neither moth nor rust consumes, and where thieves do not break in and steal. For where your treasure is, there will your heart be also".'

She closed the book and explained, 'Peter, having money doesn't make you a royal person. We can only be royal people because we have our treasure in heaven.'

As she finished, she covered me up and left me to drift off quietly to sleep. My sobs faded little by little. I curled up in a tight, foetus-like ball.

I really wanted to belong to a royal family.

3. The Animal Kingdom

I stood there, feeling a mixture of excitement and fear. I was with Mama and Papa on the other side of town, at the entrance of a formidable boarding establishment called the Industrial School. Barbed wire was strung all around the perimeter of the sprawling old building, and teachers strutted around the place, barking out orders to cowed students.

'Mama, it looks like a prison,' I wailed in dismay. 'I don't want to stay here. I want to come home with you right now.' I held tightly on to her hand.

'But, Peter, you passed the scholarship. You have to stay. It will turn you into a man.'

My father looked sterner than usual. He put his arm around my shoulders. 'Son, this is not a matter for discussion.' His tone was reproachful. 'You *will* stay and you *will* succeed. I'm not going to provide all that sausage for nothing!'

I smiled briefly, knowing that he had struck a unique bargain with the school principal. Because I had passed the required exam, half of my fees were to be paid by the government. Papa, however, had to come up with the rest. And because he had little cash, he had somehow persuaded the principal to accept, in lieu of payment, 250 pesos' worth of sausage each month.

A tiny tear ran down my face. I hugged them both tight and said I would do my best.

Mother quickly stammered out her suggestions to me.

'Don't talk back to your teachers . . . don't get into fights with the students . . . clean your teeth regularly . . . wash behind your ears . . . be a man . . . and don't forget to pray.' She then pressed a New Testament into my hand. 'Peter, don't forget to read it every day.'

A tight-lipped teacher arrived and hissed, 'Peter Asael Gonzalez, follow me.' I picked up my paper bag which contained most of the possessions of my twelve years, and waved at the receding figures of my parents. They were as upset as I was that I was leaving home. I wondered if I would ever see them again.

In my dormitory, I discovered I was to share my privacy with 150 other young men. We were all clustered in a large concrete barrack room, with beds crammed against both walls.

It was already dark, and as I unpacked I heard the unsettling sound of the boy in the next bed weeping. Heavy sobs enveloped his whole body.

'I never wanted to come to this terrible place,' he wailed.

'Nor me . . .' another followed.

Within an hour, five new boys had packed their bags and left. They were terrified of being alone at such a young age. Parents had been contacted and they departed with them.

Just as I was settling on my bed for the night, the insistent sound of a bugle outside the window startled me into sitting bolt upright again.

'What's that?'

Before I could get an answer, older boys vaulted from their beds and began to run. I followed them like a lemming, and found myself in the huge dining room. It was feeding time; nothing sinister at all.

There was no ceremony. Bits of meat and beans were plopped onto our aluminium plates by older boys, together with a chunk of French bread. I bowed my head and said grace and then began slowly eating.

'Hey, new boy, what were you doing then?'

'I was giving thanks to God for this food.'

'Are you a fanatic? A nut case?' A titter of laughter ran around my table. The boy didn't wait for a response, but wolfed down his food with the speed of everyone else.

Within five minutes, I was the only boy left in the room.

The next bewildering race was to a classroom to be addressed by the principal. We sat upright at big desks, staring with awe at an imposing figure whose eyes were underscored with pouches of weariness.

'Right, boys,' he started, clearing his throat. 'You may be very scared with what you have experienced this evening. But there is no need for fear . . . that is, if you behave yourselves.' His voice was as cold as ice.

'The first thing you need to know is that you must be up at five a.m. You will hear reveille, and I want you to jump out of your beds immediately. Once dressed, you must run downstairs and form up on the parade ground at the front of the school. You will be placed in platoons and assigned a sergeant.'

It seemed as though the man was fixing his eys directly on me.

'Some of you will be told to clean out the toilets, and others the dormitories. Those who are especially favoured will learn to march. At seven o'clock you will have breakfast. Lessons start at eight a.m. You will study until midday. After lunch you will go to the various workshops to learn different technical skills.

'Our curfew begins at ten p.m. If you are not in bed by then you will be expelled!'

After that, my mind in a whirl, I returned to the dormitory with the others and jumped fully clothed into bed. I pulled the covers over me and peeked out fearfully at my equally frightened comrades. I was afraid to go to sleep properly in case someone blew another bugle.

I had never before slept away from home, not even for one night. I kept reciting under my breath, 'Help me, God. Help me, God. I'm so scared.' All night long I was dozing in and out of twilight consciousness.

Next morning, I was quickly out of bed at the sound of the bugle. On the parade ground, because of my small stature, I was assigned to the youngest platoon.

'You tiddlers will clean out the toilets,' thundered the commanders.

But it wasn't all menial work. At that school I learned to be proud of being Mexican.

'Boys,' said the tutor, 'you belong to a civilisation that is thousands of years old, a culture which gave the New World its first university, it's first printing press, its first mint.'

My little chest swelled. I was indeed proud to be Mexican.

*　　*　　*

'Hey, Peter Asael, Bible-basher . . .' It was the older boy who had accosted me that first day in the dining-room.

'Are you crazy or something?' His voice was tinged with sarcasm, and he jerked his head to indicate the New Testament in my hands.

'What do you mean? What's wrong with reading the Bible?'

'You can't be a Catholic. We don't read the Bible. We take what the priest says. He's God's representative, you know.'

I soon realised that not only was I different in my upbringing, but also I belonged to that strange group of people labelled *Protestante*, a comparatively rare bird at that time in Mexico. It seemed as though that singled me out as someone to be ostracised.

The constant tauntings eventually became too much. I didn't have Mama close at hand to keep on reassuring me that I could be a royal person and I decided, for survival reasons, that I would have to become like the others. My language changed and deteriorated badly. I swore and told dirty stories as well as any of my companions.

One day a teacher, Mr. Garza, pulled me to one side.

'Peter, I am ashamed of you,' he scolded. 'I overheard what you just said, and I know your mother would be shocked to hear your language.'

I vowed to him that I would never use profane language again, not wanting to let my mother and father down. But on my thirteenth birthday something happened which broke my resolution.

I was deeply asleep when, at four a.m., I was grabbed from my bed by a group of giggling boys and hauled by my arms and legs out of the dormitory.

'Don't you dare scream, Gonzalez. This will be a birthday present you will never forget.'

They struggled to carry me down the staircase and over to one of the industrial buildings where students were taught to tan the hides of animals.

'Not the vat!' My voice was filled with horror as I realised what they were going to do.

'The vat it is.'

They swung me a couple of times at the side of the huge, foul-smelling tub and then let go. I sailed through the air and plopped into a noxious brown brew.

When I came up I let go a torrent of foul oaths.

'I see the Bible-basher has lost his temper again,' said José, the leader of my birthday treat committee.

It was obvious again to me that day that I had to become one of the crowd if I was to survive. We lived in a jungle and I had to learn to blend in with the animals.

I began to hang around with 'The Rabbit' and 'Blondie', two older boys who were usually up to no good. One afternoon after our technical skills lesson we were walking around the school grounds when we came across a 1941 Ford.

'That's Professor Guerrero's bone-shaker,' said The Rabbit, known as such for his protruding front teeth.

'Look, the running board's loose.' He shook it until it came away from the body of the car.

We collapsed, laughing.

'Hey,' continued Blondie, 'the tyres are too hard. Let's let out the air.' With that he pushed in the valve with a knife and the tyre was soon flat.

The pair looked at me for some action. So I produced a piece of chalk from my pocket.

'Maybe it needs a paint job,' I said, 'and possibly I can help a little.' With that I walked twice around the car, trailing the chalk around its bodywork.

They shook hands with me in delight. I was now one of them; no longer different.

The next day I was in a dream. Wow, wasn't I a tough guy! No more was I the *Protestante* sissy from the *barrio*. But I was soon to be brought down to earth: my teacher asked me to go to the principal's office, along with my two companions in crime.

I sat waiting outside the office full of dread. The others went in first and came out grinning. Maybe they weren't found out.

'Gonzalez, come in,' the principal's voice rasped out. I walked into the office.

'I'll come straight to the point.'

'Yes, sir.'

'Do you not like the paint-work on Professor Guerrero's car?' His brow furrowed, then cleared.

'Sure I do, sir.'

'Well,' his voice dripped with sarcasm, 'why did you try to change it?'

'Oh, that, sir.' I feigned surprise. 'Well, I was just about to clean it off.'

'No need for that, Gonzalez. He's already done it. Your punishment for this crime is to be on indefinite duties. You will be spending all your spare time doing menial jobs I will give you. You will not leave this campus until I say you can.' He stopped to emphasise what he had said.

'Maybe,' he continued sternly, 'that will teach you to obey, Gonzalez.'

He peered at me over his glasses. 'I'm disappointed in you, boy. I thought you came from a good home.'

I rose to my feet, trembling slightly.

The two months of forced labour were a nightmare. I was painting fences, fixing thousands of tiny stones in place on the driveway, any tiny job the principal could dream up.

After three weeks, my mother became concerned at my silence. Usually I would slip home by bus for a few hours on Saturdays and Sundays, though I was always back before curfew to sleep in my large 'cell'.

Mama looked very worried when I was ushered into a

private room at school to see her.

'Peter, what has happened?' She looked at me, puzzled. 'Why have you not been home to see us?'

Looking at her soft, sad, questioning face, I felt a sharp stab of guilt. My face grew hot with shame. Finally I began to cry.

'Come on, Peter, you must tell me.'

Out tumbled the story.

She looked at me with compassion in her eyes.

'Peter, you must remember that whatever you do in this life, you must eventually pay for it. Never forget that!'

* * *

One day there came what should have been the usual 'rumble' with the posh pupils of the Normal School, a nearby teachers' training college for wealthy kids. We called them the 'Stocking Brigade' because we considered them soft. They dubbed us the 'Sponge Dogs', because we were getting an education partly supplied by the government. They considered that sponging on the State. The enmity between the two schools regularly exploded into violence, mainly because many of the girls from their school preferred our more macho poor boys.

Despite the posh boys' scorn, many in the city of Victoria had become proud of us, because we would often stage military displays in the main soccer stadium. We would have mock battles, vault high walls, and generally show how disciplined we could be. That made the rich kids want to teach us a lesson even more.

On this particular night, the note challenging us to pitched battle with chains, brass knuckles, and sticks read, 'You sponge dogs have gone too far this time. One of our girls has been defiled by one of you and we want revenge. Meet us at the usual alley at eight p.m. Be prepared to die!'

I had previously been on five of these rumbles and, although I was scared to death, I would force myself to join in. This night we were especially well equipped. Many of the boys had been secretly making knuckle-dusters in the school workshop.

As the battle commenced, there were whoops and screams from both sides. We ran at each other like crazy people, swinging our weapons and sometimes connecting with young limbs and skulls. I was taken up with protecting myself and stayed back a little from the main part of the action.

Then from the corner of my eye, I saw one of the rich boys moving towards Porky, an overweight boy from our school who really shouldn't have been in the battle. He was too slow to escape trouble. I saw the flash of something metallic, and a large knife was thrust into his left side. Blood began to spurt as his assailant ran desperately to escape retaliation.

'Porky . . .' I gasped, running over to his sprawled body. I opened up his shirt and saw a deep wound. His face was an ashen grey, his lips were faintly blue, and he was breathing fast. The choking sound in his throat terrified me.

The battle ended as quickly as it had begun. We managed to haul the semiconscious Porky to a nearby Red Cross post, where the officer in charge stitched him up without an anaesthetic. Porky yelped in pain, but the stern-faced man, even though he saw the boy's baffled, frightened face, didn't feel he deserved pity. He guessed how the wound had come about.

We carried Porky back to school, without telling any of the staff, but by the next morning he had a high fever. Scared, a deputation of us decided to tell the principal what had happened. Porky was rushed to the hospital and at last given the care he'd needed.

José, who had also been on the rumble, turned to me as the ambulance sped down the school drive. 'It could be you or me next, Peter.'

I laughed bitterly. 'I suppose so. Bit I'll tell you something, José, my mother was wrong. We are *not* special people. We are animals. It's a jungle we live in, and only the fittest will survive.'

My voice rose, bewildered and bitter.

'I'm going to do anything to survive . . . *anything*!'

4. In the Footsteps of a Prophet?

It was going to be a day to remember. After graduating as a mechanical technician, I had left the Industrial School and had been offered a job working in one of the large factories of Monterrey, a huge industrial city of 1,500,000 people, located about 170 miles from Victoria. As I was soon earning good money, I'd decided that I should become the breadwinner for my family. My father's eyesight had become so bad that it was almost impossible for him to drive the bus any more.

I was whistling at the top of my voice as I turned to cross the bridge to our little *barrio* in Victoria. The sun, a huge crimson ball, was fast sinking below the horizon and I felt at peace with the world. Then I spotted Ruben, my ten-year-old brother. He was hurling huge rocks at our front door, and his face was full of hate and anger.

I stopped in astonishment, and slipped into the doorway of the Fixed Price Store. Surely, my kid brother couldn't be doing something so stupid!

But rock after rock slammed against our door.

I broke into a run and jumped on him from behind, grabbing the next missile and twisting his arm up behind his back.

'Hey, Ruben, what are you doing? Stop it!'

There was a high colour in his cheeks.

'Let go of my arm,' he complained fiercely. 'You're hurting me.'

'Not until you tell me what you are up to.'

We went to the side of the road and sat down in the dirt, and Ruben sobbed out the story.

'Mama won't give me any pocket money.' His voice rose to an angry, tearful shout. 'I feel so poor. I get so humiliated because I can't buy things like other kids . . .'

I put my arm around him, sympathising at once with his predicament.

'I understand. You don't want to be different from the other kids. But don't you see that Mama has no money to give to you. We are a poor family.'

'But –' he choked, 'I don't want to be poor. I hate it!'

I lifted Ruben to his feet and we headed into the house. Mama looked furious as she faced her rebel son. 'Your father will hear of this. He will punish you.' Her finger prodded his shoulder, giving emphasis to each word.

Papa shuffled in through the damaged front door a few minutes later. Mama whispered in his ear what had happened.

'I'll teach you a lesson, young man.' Papa's voice was hard and angry. 'I'm going to spank you so hard that you won't forget it in a hurry.'

Ruben didn't wait for his punishment. He dashed through the back door and vaulted a fence into the next yard. My father hadn't a chance to catch him.

'Don't think you'll get away with this,' Papa yelled after the fleeing figure. 'I can wait.'

We went to bed early that night, and later I heard the anguished cries of Ruben. He had tried to tiptoe back into the house and up to his bedroom when my father had caught him and punished him with his strap. My heart went out to him, and the resolve which I hadn't yet revealed to my family was strengthened.

'Goodnight, brother,' I murmured. 'At least your punishment is now over. You have nothing to fear. If you are brave I will give you some good news in the morning to make up for your pain.'

*   *   *

There were now eight children in the family, the last – baby Ricardo – just one month old. My mother looked more and more tired as the days went by, and I'd been worrying about her and my father for some time. There was a lot to cope with in Victoria. Hurricanes threatened the community regularly, and a recent one had destroyed many homes. Mother thanked God that only part of our wall was damaged, but another time we might not escape so lightly. I determined to put my proposition to the family the very next day.

That morning, Cesar joined us from the Industrial School. He had spent a year there already, and seemed to have grown up a lot.

'You don't look thirteen,' I said as I stood back from hugging him in welcome.

He thanked me, as gentle as ever. 'I really love it there, Peter. I play the bugle in the band, you know.'

Bursting to reveal my plan to them all, I suggested we go out for a treat – a soda pop at the Fixed Price Store.

As we walked the short way along the street, Cesar commented on the nickname I'd had at the school. 'Everyone there still calls you Asael, the Prophet.'

That really struck home because I hadn't been much of a prophet during my stay at the school. And I daren't tell my parents of my behaviour since in Monterrey, where I was chain-smoking and drinking way beyond my capabilities each night after my shift in the factory.

We sipped our soda pop and I held Mama's hand.

'I have a suggestion for you all,' I began. They listened eagerly. 'It will mean your lives will change. Are you ready for that?'

'Of course . . . if it is God's will.'

Why did Mama have to bring God into everything! I bit my lip so I wouldn't say anything to hurt her.

'Well, I want you all to come and live in Monterrey. I have a good job and I can now support you all. We could find a house there and all share it. We could be one big family again. What do you say?'

Mama and Papa exchanged glances, their eyes alight

with excitement.

'We would be honoured to come.' Mother looked at me with a smile that would melt any son's heart.

I knew I would have to consider getting on the royal road again, and that might be difficult. But it was a risk I had to take. I wanted so much for Papa and Maria to be close to me again.

'What do you think, Cesar?' He seemed happy.

'Sounds fine to me. Maybe I could get a job there when I finish at the school. Do you know that next year I'm taking the same course as you did?' He threw back his head and laughed. 'I'm following in the Prophet's footsteps!'

*　　*　　*

'Hey, Gonzalez, you'll have to clean up your face a bit when your parents come.'

The din of the music from the juke box was making my head spin in that run-down bar. Or was it the beer? As a sixteen-year-old trying to be a man, I was endeavouring to match the hard-drinking prowess of my colleagues in the Monterrey factory.

'That's not dirt . . .' My voice trailed off. I tried to collect my thoughts as my head began to whirl again . . . or was it the room moving?

'I'm growing a moustache, you idiots. That's not dirt.'

Owl-eyed, I tried to focus on my watch.

'Hey, do you realise it's five in the morning?' I shredded a cigarette into the ash-tray in front of me.

'Who cares, Gonzalez. Have another beer. You've only had fifteen . . .'

The strange thing about this was that I wasn't enjoying the experience. I had lost my dignity. I was ashamed, yet I didn't know how to break free from the grip of my colleagues. When my family came to join me, I stopped drinking for a short time . . . a very short time.

I knew that something vital was missing from my life. Maybe it was romance. One night I dreamed that I had found someone special. She had dark hair, wonderful hazel eyes, and the face of a child. She was terribly fragile. And terribly beautiful. She was to be my wife!

I couldn't get that face out of my mind. After my shift, I would go to a quiet bar in another part of town, sit in a corner with an ample supply of beer, and weep. The more I drank, the more I wept. Great, tearing sobs seemed to be trying to rip me apart.

Sometimes a bar hostess would come over to me.

'What's the matter, honey? Can I help?'

'Please go away. I want to be alone.'

When my crying became unbearable, I would finally stagger to my feet and head for our house like a homing pigeon. I would hope my parents were long asleep and wouldn't see me in such a pitiful condition.

One night I almost fell through the doorway. In the darkness I started to feel my way towards my bedroom, my hands held out in front of me. But then I froze when I saw, through a crack in her bedroom door, the figure of my mother on her knees.

'Lord, please help Peter. Please heal him from this drinking. Please save him . . .' She repeated this time and time again, desperation in her voice. I was her eldest son, and she was seeing me fall apart in front of her eyes. I had left her royal highway and was heading for trouble.

Her words rang in my ears as I fell, fully-clothed, on to my creaky bed. In my drunken stupor, I had the recurring vision of Mama on her knees for me.

'My God,' I finally cried out, 'what am I doing like this? Please help me.'

5. 'Are You in Love?'

'*Ay, mamacita!*' (My goodness, little mother!)

'What's up, Peter? What did you see?' asked Rogelio, who worked with me in the same factory. He lit another cigarette as we sat in a little *barrio* park in Monterrey on a Sunday morning in 1947.

'Look at those two angels approaching. Have you ever seen anything so beautiful in all your life?'

As the teenage girls, both with skin like silk, and dressed alike in red-and-white polka-dot dresses, came by the bench where we were sitting, I whistled at them.

They ignored me completely. That is the usual way in Mexico when a young man tries to flirt. Girls are expected to walk with their eyes downcast, and those who smile freely may be suspected of being flippant and flirtatious. But often their apparent lack of interest only means, 'Try again.'

So I did!

'Hey, little ones, you are so pretty!'

They were both petite and slender, and they cast disdainful looks at me in unison. So I fell in step with them.

'Why,' I said, flicking an ash from my cigarette to the ground, 'won't you speak to me?'

Each word I said made them increase their pace even more, until they were almost running. Finally they disappeared into a cream-coloured building which I recognised as the local evangelical church. Only then did I realise that they'd had Bibles clasped tightly in their hands. I guess I had at first thought they were holding handbags.

Crowds were milling around the church. Should I join them? No, I had cigarette smoke on my breath and that would be embarrassing. I always had an excuse why I shouldn't enter the House of God.

When I got back to the park, Rogelio, seeing my dreamy expression, asked, 'Were you successful?'

'I think I could have been, but they suddenly went into a church and that was the last I saw of them.'

'Oh, that must have been that crazy Protestant church. Forget them, they are just fanatics.' He gestured contemptuously. 'Be patient, Peter, there will be other girls.'

Although I was joking and laughing with my friend, all I could think of was those girls, especially the face of the younger one. 'Maybe she is the girl in my dream . . .'

When I returned home, I went straight to my room, locked the door, drew the curtain and turned off all the lights. I lay on the bed in complete darkness and switched on the radio. Mexicans love romantic music and I am no exception. But now all the mushy words that I usually laughed at took on a new meaning. Rhymes about 'moon' and 'June' didn't seem so crazy after all. I applied the words I heard over the crackling radio to the pretty one I had followed in the street. If only I could meet her again!

'I'd even go to church for her,' I eventually conceded.

That night in the bar, I somehow couldn't drink as I usually did. I had only four beers. In that darkened tavern, I kept closing my eyes and conjuring up the face of the girl.

*   *   *

Ronaldo worked in the same factory as I did. Being blond, he didn't look Mexican at all. He lived just across the road from me, and one day invited me in to meet Lidia, his wife.

As we sipped tea, she kept staring at me, a look of puzzlement on her face. I began to feel uncomfortable, feeling that possibly horns were growing out of the top of my head.

'Is there a problem?' I finally asked Lidia.

'No, it's just that your face seems familiar, Peter. I've got

48

it! Did you once live in Victoria City?'

'Yes, that's right.'

'And did you go to a Presbyterian church there?'

'Yes.'

'And is your full name Peter Asael Gonzalez?'

'Yes.'

'Well, you will remember my father. He was the pastor there.'

'Oh . . .'

'Do you go to church now, Peter?'

There was an awkward pause, then I blurted out, 'I'm afraid not.'

She pounced. 'Well, why don't you come along to our new church?'

I resented her pushiness, but I managed a weak smile. 'I'll think about it.'

She didn't pursue the matter on this occasion, but each time I went into her home she would again invite me to visit her church. Over the months, she grew large with pregnancy – in Mexico we have the expression that she had become 'ill with child' – and I felt increasingly bad about my excuses for not taking up her invitation.

'Peter, look, we have a quartet coming to sing for us this Sunday from the United States. Why don't you come? I'm sure you would enjoy them.'

I gave in. 'O.K., Lidia, you have talked me into it. Just this once, though. Where is the church?'

She described it, and I gasped as I realised it was the one into which the girl of my dreams had disappeared.

On the Sunday evening, I slipped late into service so I wouldn't be recognised, and found a seat at the back of the packed building. The Gospel music was beautiful, but all I was interested in was looking for the girl. Even during the sermon, I cut off my mind from the words the evangelist spoke and let my eyes wander around the sanctuary. There was no sign of her. When the altar call was made, I slipped out and into the street. I was bitterly disappointed that I hadn't seen her.

The next night I felt an irresistible urge to go back for the second evening of this week of meetings. I got to the church early this time and managed to sit near the front. Then I spotted the dark flowing hair of the girls a couple of rows ahead of me. My heart started to pound; but which was the one in my dreams? They looked almost like twins!

Each night I was in my seat well before the meeting started and they, too, were in their same seats. At the end of the last service, I was almost despairing of meeting them when Lidia came over to me. I had also been attending the Sunday School, and she had decided that I had by now earned an official introduction to some of the girls there. After an age of hand-shaking, I was finally introduced to 'my cousins, Hilda and Blanca.' Both smiled, showing beautiful teeth, and I stammered out, 'How do you do?'

My mind was in a whirl, and I still couldn't figure out which was which.

I could not concentrate on my work that week, and the next Sunday couldn't come around quickly enough. As I prepared at last to go to the service, my mother commented on how smart I looked. I had let my appearance go so much over the previous year that she was pleasantly surprised.

'Are you going to church again, Peter?'

I beamed.

'You make me very happy.'

The church was filling up rapidly when I took my seat near the front. But where were the girls? They did not come. I was so disappointed.

After the service, I called to Lidia, 'Hey, where are your cousins?'

'Oh, they have gone away on a two-month vacation to Tampico.'

'But that's four hundred miles away. How can I see them?'

'Why do you want to see them?'

I ignored the question.

*　　*　　*

I was clocking in for work when I cast a cursory glance at

the factory notice board. There I saw a poster which said, 'TRIP TO TAMPICO. Sign up now.' I decided on the spot, and was one of the first to register.

The bus journey to Tampico, a Gulf of Mexico port, took more than six hours. We arrived late at night and had to sleep in the bus. I could hardly wait for morning, so I could rush off to the beach. At nine a.m. I ran towards the golden sands and began walking along the edge of the shore. Even though it was early, there were thousands of people already on the beach. How could I possibly find them amid such crowds?

But suddenly I spotted them, playing volleyball. I nervously walked past them as if I hadn't noticed them. The sand crunched agreeably beneath my feet as I walked. My mind went blank. What could I use as an excuse for being there? It looked as if I were following them around. Well, I was, so why should I hide it?

After a few yards, I headed back, and then I half-walked, half-ran towards them. My heart was hammering in my chest.

'*Hola*' (Hello). I waved breathlessly to the two of them.

Both smiled, but Blanca, the younger of the two, turned her deep hazel eyes to mine and held them for a split second.

'Would you like to play volleyball with us?' she whispered.

She was the one! The girl of my dreams!

'I would, very much.' Blanca turned her ripe, soft mouth towards me, then smiled shyly.

My legs went to jelly and my stomach began to flutter.

Before I started playing, I spoke to her mother.

'Hi, do you remember me? I go to your church in Monterrey.' She nodded.

After a few games, Blanca's sister went off to buy some soda pop and we flopped down together on the golden sand.

'How do you like church?' she asked.

'Oh, I love it. I love the music. I love seeing you there.'

Her face flushed. She was so slight! She looked as if I

51

could crush her in the palm of my hand.

I spent the happiest day of my life with Blanca. It ended when Mario, her brother, who had been hovering nearby, told her that she and her sister had to go back to their holiday home. I formally shook hands with my wife-to-be, with her sister, mother and brother.

'I hope to see you in Monterrey very soon,' I said eagerly to Blanca.

She lowered her eyes in a timid way. I felt my face turning scarlet. I wanted to blow her a kiss, but held back.

I skipped back to the bus, then broke into a run as I realised I was late. Breathlessly, I clambered aboard.

'I'm sorry I am late, but I was lost,' I told the others.

'Are you in love, Peter?' asked one of them.

'Could be my friends,' I said, the colour rising in my cheeks, 'could be.'

6. Performance

It was midnight when I scurried breathlessly up the stairs to my bedroom. I was still in a daze after my day in Tampico. Then I heard the muffled sounds of someone jumping around in the bedroom.

I flung open the door and found the strange figure of a young man, dressed like Elvis Presley, cavorting around in front of the mirror. He was singing, 'You ain't nothing but a hound dog . . .' in broken English.

'Elvis' stopped in his tracks when he saw my reflection, and turned to look at me. His lips quivered like those of the King of Rock and Roll, and his hair was slicked in the same fashion.

'Hi, Peter, what do you think of the outfit?' A grin blossomed on his face.

It was Ruben! But what was he doing in my room? He was supposed to be in Victoria at the Industrial School.

Then I spotted Cesar, huddled under the covers of my bed.

'He doesn't like my music,' chuckled Ruben.

'Hey, my brother,' I punched Cesar affectionately on the shoulder. It was the first time I'd seen him since his graduation. 'It's great to see you again, but what is Ruben doing here as well?'

Cesar grinned broadly as he gave me an *abrazo* (a hug) in greeting.

'Oh, he was awful during his first year. He got bad marks for discipline and didn't like the school at all. I don't think he will be going back. He wants to complete his education here in Monterrey.'

They looked at me and, obviously, caught the sparkle in my eyes.

'Hey,' whistled Ruben. 'I haven't seen you look so happy for a long time. What's wrong?'

'When you grow up you'll understand,' I replied mysteriously. 'I'm in love. I've met a girl at church and –'

'Church?' Cesar laughed in disbelief. 'Don't tell me you're going to church again. I can't remember the last time I went.'

'Oh.' I was embarrassed. 'I only go because of the girl. She's so beautiful.'

After nearly five hours of chit-chat, we all finally agreed to go to sleep and continue the conversation next morning. I let my brothers use my bed and I rolled myself up in some spare bedclothes on the floor.

* * *

I was fascinated with the garish lights patterning the sky and the loud music of the travelling fair now in our *barrio* park. We were all warned by the pastor not to have anything to do with such sinful amusement, especially on a Sunday.

'This is the Lord's day,' he insisted. 'Keep it holy.'

I managed to slip by the side of Blanca as she came out of church that night. It was getting dark as the dusk deepened in the evening sky, and I knew that this was the night I had to make my move. For weeks I had tried to summon up the courage to ask her to be my regular girlfriend. But somehow the words would clam up in my mouth.

Finally, I took a deep breath, and blurted out my request.

'Peter, you know I can't go there tonight. You heard what the pastor said. It would be wrong for us to go.'

'But –'

'Peter, I'm sorry.'

I had to think fast.

'I understand. But would you mind if I stood with you for

54

a while outside the pastor's house? We could watch the lights from there and talk a little?'

She smiled.

'O.K.' Her eyes were sparkling. Her endearing shyness grabbed at my heart. Normally I had no problems in chatting with the girls of my neighbourhood. I prided myself on my silver tongue. But with Blanca, I almost dried up. My slick phrases seemed cheap with her.

After a few minutes of embarrassed silence outside the pastor's house I turned to her and said, 'Blanca, I have something very serious to say to you.'

'What is it?'

'I want you to be my girlfriend. What do you say?'

'I . . . I will have to think about it.' Her voice faltered.

'What is there to think about?' I looked at her questioningly. 'I can't wait any longer. I've been wanting to ask you for some time now but have never had the courage.'

'Let me think a while.'

I stood staring at the flashing, twinkling lights of the fair for what seemed like an eternity.

Then she squeezed my hand.

'O.K., Peter. I'll be your girlfriend.'

It was the greatest moment of my seventeen years of life. I was speechless. I stood in a state of happy shock for nearly ten minutes.

'Are you sure?' I finally asked her.

'Of course I am. You will be my boyfriend.'

In many countries that answer would have meant that we could have begun our private courtship together. But in our society a boy and girl are not allowed to go out together without a chaperon before marriage. In Blanca's case, that meant reporting to her mother that we wished to spend some time together, and she would then assign a member of the family to be with us. Usually it was Hilda, the one-year-older 'twin', and although she was in sympathy with our romance, we still didn't feel really free with her. Holding hands, for instance, was completely out of the question.

I began to think of ways to see her, unhindered.

Eventually I devised a daring plan to go over to her school, which nestled in the shadow of El Obispado (the Bishop's Palace). This was on a hill overlooking the city, and provided an excellent view of the Monterrey. By now, I owned a new motor-cycle, and would meet Blanca at the school gates. We went together to the top of the hill and shared our sandwiches. Even in that relatively safe place, I didn't have the courage to hold her hand.

Another way I knew I could be with her was to attend every service at the church. I even went to the women's meetings so that I could see her there.

One day Mario, Blanca's elder brother, shared a soda pop with me in a nearby store, after Sunday evening service.

'Peter,' he looked at me very seriously. 'What do you think about church?'

I was taken aback.

'It's O.K. for meeting people.'

'But you don't feel anything about Christ?'

'No, I don't feel anything. Nothing at all.'

'That is strange.' He looked surprised. 'You seem such a different person these days. Much more gentle. I thought maybe you had been "born again".'

I got a perverse pleasure from his words. I knew I had become a good play actor; I had obviously fooled him.

*　　*　　*

'Peter, guess who's come back to our church?'

'Who?'

'The Harvesters, the quartet who sang the first time we met. They will be here for a week of meetings.'

It was then that I realised that twelve months had elapsed since I had been attending the church. A year in which I should have been given an Oscar for my performance as a pretend Christian. I had even fooled the pastor, who accepted me as a member of the church and appointed me president of the youth department. I still had a nagging fear, however, that this big act was going to catch up with

56

me one day but, for now, nobody questioned me about it.

When The Harvesters arrived, I volunteered to be their tour guide. I took them and Rene Zapata, an evangelist from Guatemala, up to the top of El Obispado and later showed them the 5,700-foot mountain, Cerro de la Silla (Saddle Mountain), which dominates our industrial city.

I explained that the centre of town was Zaragoza Plaza, selected in 1612 as the site for a new city after disastrous floods wiped out much of the original one.

'Once a colonial plaza of great renown,' I read from the guide book, 'it was renovated some years ago and given a more functional design. But it is still the gathering place for old and young. On Thursday and Sunday nights, there are concerts, and strolling around the plaza is the thing to do – unless you sit on a bench and survey the promenade.'

The first evening of the week of meetings was quite an event. There was an electric atmosphere in the air, and the church was packed to the doors. The music was heavenly. I loved American Gospel quartet music, but I didn't really listen to the words.

Then Rene Zapata got up to speak. I let my mind wander a little, thinking of the day when Blanca and I could be married and I wouldn't have to go through this pretence any more.

Mr. Zapata looked at the congregation with fierce dark eyes, and said, 'Every one of you will have to go to hell if you don't accept Christ!' I sat up and began to listen.

'You can play games with yourself, but not with God. He knows all about you. He isn't fooled!'

The Latin evangelist paused for a moment. Then he looked straight at me and I squirmed. I suddenly found myself tense, unable to sit still.

'Are *you* playing games, young man? Do you want to spend eternity in hell?'

I became frightened. That would mean that I would be separated from my beloved Blanca forever. But worse than that I would not know God.

A tear began to trickle down my face and splashed onto my New Testament. I had it open at a verse he had just

57

read. It was Revelation 20:15, 'And if anyone's name was not found written in the Book of Life, he was thrown into the lake of fire.'

I knew my name was not there. The feeling of disquiet intensified. Another tear splashed down. I could have kicked myself because I had projected the image of being very macho. Now here I was making a fool of myself.

Suddenly the individual tears became a torrent. My face was wet with tears. I didn't hear anymore. I just closed my eyes and tried to stem the flow of tears, but they wouldn't be stopped. I put my head in my hands and cried like a baby.

Then I felt a hand on my shoulder. The message was over and so was the service. It was the preacher.

'What is the matter, Peter? Why are you crying? When you showed us around the town, you were such a happy-go-lucky person.'

'I know,' I sobbed, a feeling of self-loathing welling up in me, 'but that was all a pretence. It wasn't real. My name isn't written in the Book of Life. I know it isn't.'

He listened with understanding.

'Do you want it to be, Peter?'

'I do. More than anything.'

Rene took me into the vestry and began sharing with me how he had become a Christian.

'I played games for years, Peter, just as you have been doing. But then I had to face up to the fact that I was a sinner and was going to hell. I asked Jesus to forgive my sins and He did. He changed my life and saved me.'

I told Rene that I wanted the same experience.

'O.K., Peter, but I want you to make your commitment in public. I want you to do it as a witness to everyone still left in the church.'

I knew that would be a humiliating experience for me. After all, they thought I was already a Christian.

Rene led me by the arm back into the sanctuary. There was a hush as we went over to a group who that night had accepted Christ.

'Peter, I want you to kneel down and ask Jesus to forgive

your sins and save you from hell!; to give you a new life.'

With tears streaming like a river, I asked Jesus to do these things. I must have been on my knees for ten minutes.

When I got up, the Guatemalan evangelist hugged me close.

'Welcome to God's royal family.'

I shook hands with the other new Christians and then, out of the corner of my eye, I saw the slight figure of Blanca. She stood in a corner watching me.

As our eyes met, she waved, a tear on her delicate cheek.

'I'm so happy,' she mouthed. 'So happy . . .'

7. 'God Told Me To Do It'

I looked across from my factory lathe at Javier, a young man with a handsome, craggy face and a macho appearance.

'Hey, Javier, did you have a good weekend?'

'Sure.'

'What did you do?'

'I . . . I . . .' The words died in his throat.

'I hope you did nothing you are ashamed of,' I shouted so he could hear me above the clatter of the machinery.

I saw him take a deep breath.

'Peter,' he said sadly, 'I want to make a confession to you. I want to tell you that I am a Christian and I would like you to come to church with me next Sunday.'

His confession was like a knife stabbing at my heart. He didn't know that I, too, was a Christian. What a poor witness both of us had given in the factory.

'Javier,' I said, no less embarrassed than he had been. 'I also have a confession to make to you. I have been a believer for the past six months. I feel so ashamed that you have not seen Christ in my life.'

After my conversion, I had thrown myself headlong into the church activities, and spent hours at the various meetings studying the Scriptures and praying. Always Blanca was at my side. But when I came to work, I just froze. I somehow found it impossible to witness to my hard-drinking friends. I had stopped going to the sleazy bars with them, but they just assumed it was because I now had a girlfriend and she was taking up all my time.

'Javier, I believe God has used you today to tell me not to be ashamed of Him and His Gospel. For that is what I've been, up to now.'

I asked my friend why he had suddenly made his confession.

'It was because the pastor in our church last night preached on Luke 9:26.'

Before he could go any further the siren signalled the end of the shift. He quickly gathered up his lunch box, but before he left, he shouted, 'Why don't you read that verse when you get home, *brother*?'

'I will, thank you.'

I couldn't get up to my bedroom fast enough. I opened my Bible and leafed through the wafer-thin pages until I came to the verse he had mentioned.

It read, 'For whoever is ashamed of me and of my words, of him will the Son of man be ashamed when he comes in his glory and the glory of the Father and of the holy angels.'

I sank to my knees. 'Lord,' I prayed, 'I confess that I have been ashamed of you before my workmates. But now I want to be strong in you. I want to preach to them, not only in words, but also through my very life.'

Next day, I saw my workmates in a new light. I could see the masks on their faces. They were desperately afraid to reveal their real selves. So I began to witness to them, but it was received mainly with mocking.

'Hey, Gonzalez has seen the light. He's gone bonkers.'

I wasn't hurt by the words. I just felt pity for them, for they were hiding the terrible longings in their own hearts. I loved these people who were now persecuting me unmercifully.

'Maybe God is taking your prayer seriously,' said Blanca when I told her of what had been happening.

*   *   *

'Peter, there is a phone call for you in the shop.' We didn't have a phone, but the corner shop would allow theirs to be used for incoming calls for those who gave them regular business.

I followed the little boy who had brought me the message and lifted the receiver. Blanca's voice greeted me.

'Peter, I have something to tell you.'

'What is it? What's wrong?' She sounded upset.

'My father has just had a heart attack. He has died.' Her voice cracked.

'I'll be right over.'

As soon as I reached her home, the family's suffering communicated itself to me. They mourned aloud, and I found myself weeping with them. A torrent of emotions overwhelmed me. It struck me for the first time how fragile life was, how quickly it could be over. As I tried to comfort Blanca, I realised that my own life wasn't going to last for ever. I felt a new urgency to learn about God's plan for my life, and to study His Word.

Shortly afterwards I was scanning a Christian newspaper a visitor had left in my home. As I flicked through the pages, I found little that really interested me. But then I saw, tucked away at the bottom of the back page, a small advertisement which said, 'The Bible Seminary announces its second year of Bible Studies. Enrol now.' It gave a box number in Puebla, a city eighty miles south of Mexico City.

I took the paper up to my room and began to pray.

'Lord, I need your confirmation right now whether or not I should go to this seminary. I am going to open your Word now and I ask you to please speak to me through it.'

My Bible was already well-worn from study. I had enrolled in a part-time Bible school in Monterrey and attended classes in between my work shifts. But now I wondered if God were calling me to full-time study.

I searched the Scriptures for several minutes, but could not find a verse that seemed to fit my situation.

'Lord,' I said desperately, as I placed the Bible on my lap, 'I am serious about this. Please speak to me now.'

I again began flicking the pages, when suddenly I came to Matthew 10:37 and 38. I read, 'He who loves father or mother more than me is not worthy of me; and he who loves son or daughter more than me is not worthy of me; and he who does not take his cross and follow me is not worthy of me.'

'But, Lord,' I argued as the words sank in. 'I am the main breadwinner in this house. What will happen to my family if I leave? Will they suffer? Then there is Blanca. We are now engaged to be married. It seems crazy just to get up and leave her at this time.'

I sat there quietly for a moment and decided I must talk to the family and Blanca. I will go only if they raise no objections,' I told God. 'That will be my fleece to you.'

With trepidation I grabbed the newspaper and headed out to the *sala* (living room). I found my father stretched out on the couch having an afternoon siesta. Mother was sitting quietly in a corner reading her Bible.

I shook my father gently and whispered, 'Papa, wake up. Can I have a word with you on the balcony?'

Papa eased himself back to consciousness and rubbed his eyes. 'Of course, my son.' He cleared sleep from his throat, and squinted at a nearby clock. Then he followed me to the balcony.

I showed him the advertisement and he screwed up his seeing eye to try to comprehend what it said.

'What is it? A Bible seminary?'

'That's right, Papa. I think God is calling me to go there.'

He said nothing.

'What do you think?' I urged.

He took my arm and held it tight. 'Peter, if you have decided to go and you want to go, just do it. I will be glad to help you in any way I can, even though you know our circumstances. Whatever I can do, I'll do it for you.'

'Thank you, Papa.'

Mother had been straining her ears to hear our conversation.

'What's this about you going to seminary, Peter?'

I showed her the advertisement.

'Peter, if you go we may not have as much food as we would like, but on the other hand you will be fed with the Word of Life.' She smiled. 'I want you to go to seminary because I know God has called you to be a minister. He wants you to serve Him. I have wanted this for a long time.'

Now came the biggest hurdle. What was I going to say to Blanca? How would she respond? That day she was helping out as cashier at her brother Mario's shop, and I went straight there.

'Blanca,' I began, having found a private corner in which to speak to her. 'Please don't get mad at me. I love you very much. And what I am going to do is not because I don't love you.'

She gasped.

'Not another girl! You don't have another than me? She is not going to have your baby . . . oh, no . . .!' Her face drained as pale as milk.

'Please, Blanca,' I said raising my hand, 'listen to me.'

She put her face in her hands and sobbed helplessly.

'Don't tell me you have another girl . . .' The conversation was getting out of hand.

'Blanca,' I cut in urgently, 'I WANT TO GO TO SEMINARY!'

There was a momentary silence.

'You what? But I thought . . .'

'I know what you thought, but you were wrong. I love you and I will come back.'

She threw her arms around me, a very un-Mexican gesture, and said, 'Peter, I want you to go to seminary. That is, as long as we can be together when you have finished. I want us to serve God together.'

Her sobs subsided, but all at once she seemed terribly fragile. And terribly beautiful. I looked at her slight figure and said, 'Blanca, I love you so much that I am going to give you a new name.'

'What is it?'

'From now I will call you *Chiquita* (little one). You will always be my little one.'

*   *   *

A confused little group gathered at the Monterrey bus terminal exactly one week later to wave me off. Mexicans are renowned for expressing their emotions freely, and our parting on this occasion was no exception. The tears flowed profusely, but mingled with them was a sense of pride and gladness. No one doubted the rightness of my step.

The twelve-hour journey seemed interminable. I knew that I was breaking through another barrier just as I had when I had first left my *barrio* in Victoria City, and then again when I'd gone to the Industrial School. But this was the biggest and most frightening yet.

I felt in my pocket and fished out 28 pesos.

'Lord,' I whispered, 'you know that this is all I own in the world. I'm going to trust you to provide for me at the seminary.'

I didn't even have the address of the college in Puebla, just the box number. Also, I hadn't made any application for a place there. What if they wouldn't accept me? What if they demanded the fees in advance? I didn't know what to do when we arrived at the bustling commercial centre, famous for its coloured tiles and onyx. There were lots of people milling round the bus station, but no one had heard of the college.

Finally, I went outside and got in a taxi and asked the driver to take me to the nearest Protestant church. When I arrived there, the caretaker was locking up.

'I'm sorry,' he said, studying the advertisement, 'I've never heard of this place. It must be new.'

I was just about to leave when he called after me, 'Hey, we have some Americans working here at the church. Maybe they will know about the place.' He directed me to their house and I knocked on the door. It was opened by a large familiar figure.

'Peter,' he shouted in delight. 'What are you doing here?'

The others crowded around him, and I found myself face to face with The Harvesters quartet.

We had a wonderful time. Not only did they know where the seminary was, but they asked me to stay with them. They sang some of their songs and I sang solos with their backing. A new injection of confidence buoyed me up.

The next day, two of The Harvesters took me across to the brand-new building that housed the seminary.

'Name?' the registrar greeted me officiously.

'Gonzalez, sir. Peter Asael Gonzalez.'

He checked through his records and shook his head. 'I'm afraid we have no record of your application, Mr. Gonzalez.'

'Yes, I know that. I haven't applied yet!'

'I beg your pardon. You can't come to seminary without filling in the proper application forms.'

'But God told me to come,' I protested.

He looked at me in utter astonishment.

8. The 'Red Sea' Opens Up

I sat numb with amazement as I listened to the three students talk about how they were nearly lynched for their faith.

'We went to this small town in the next state and were going from door to door sharing our faith in Jesus Christ,' explained Raul, a fresh-faced teenager in his second year.

'All of a sudden the three of us heard the bell tolling in the local Catholic church.'

The Catholic priest had apparently incited a mob to attack them because he didn't want Protestants preaching 'another gospel' in his town.

'Before we knew it, we were surrounded by an angry crowd, most of the people carrying rocks. They herded us into the main square and told us that we were to be stoned to death.'

I put my hand over my mouth as the student continued, an edge of steel in his voice now. 'We were willing to lay down our lives for Him, but just then, an evangelical family from the town appeared and shouted at the mob to stop. They grabbed our hands and we ran with them to their nearby home, chased all the way. We had to hide there for hours before managing finally to escape.'

This was an ugly side of being a Christian that I had not encountered before. It seemed incredible that one group of so-called believers had tried to murder another and – to make it worse – in the name of God. That was terrible!

Did that mean that I, too, might be called on one day to lay down my life for Christ? It dawned on me that I could easily be the victim of a lynch-mob or a sniper's bullet in this cauldron we know as Latin America. A trickle of fear entered my mind. Had I done the right thing to come as a student to the seminary? This new life could prove to be more dangerous than even those boyhood rumbles with my friends at the Industrial School!

I had been questioned carefully by the North American registrar when I first arrived. He was puzzled why I had not applied to go to my denomination's seminary.

'Sir, I have come to realise that the problems of the world are so vast that I should not be tied to one denomination,' I told him. 'I want to serve the whole Body of Christ and I think I can do that better if I attend a non-denominational college like yours.'

He scrutinised the form I had just filled in and noted that I had qualifications from the Industrial School and a successful career in the Monterrey factory.

'Why do you want to give up your career? You certainly won't make much money as a preacher. What is your motivation?'

I took my Bible and boldly asked if he would listen to a reading that had become my reason for coming to the college.

It was from Luke 4, when Jesus returned to Nazareth where he had been brought up. Jesus went to the synagogue on the Sabbath day, and read the following from Isaiah: 'The Spirit of the Lord is upon me, because he has annointed me to preach good news to the poor. He has sent me to proclaim release to the captives and recovering of sight to the blind, to set at liberty those who are oppressed, to proclaim the acceptable year of the Lord.'

I looked up at the registrar. 'I believe that is exactly what I should be doing with my life. I have seen much injustice done in my *barrio* and also in the factory. Not only by the rich to the poor, but also by the poor to the poor. If a man can take advantage of his fellow man, he will. It isn't just money that is needed, but a change inside. I found it when I came to Christ and I now want to proclaim the 'acceptable year of the Lord'. I want to help set free those who are oppressed because I know God is for justice.'

I could see my two friends from The Harvesters were thrilled with my response. 'Bravo, bravo, Peter,' one of them clapped.

'O.K., Mr. Gonzalez.' The registrar seemed impressed. 'We have talked of money and the way you have decided that it is not of primary importance. But here we have a problem. It takes money to run this school. Do you have enough to pay your fees and support yourself?'

I shook my head.

'No, I don't, and I don't know how it is going to come. God told me I had to come. He's going to supply the fees, I know that.'

He pushed his glasses to the edge of his nose and pondered the situation briefly. Then he looked straight at me and said, 'All right, Peter, we will trust God with you for the next three months, but if the money doesn't come in by then, we will have no alternative but to assume that God is not in this and we will have to ask you to leave.'

I agreed.

The next three months were idyllic. I loved the lessons and especially enjoyed being given a little adobe-style mission church, made of mud bricks and straw, to run. It was in Zacatelco, a sleepy village some thirty miles from Puebla. Even for me, the place with its traditional square plaza, around which were grouped some shabby public buildings, was quaint. The twentieth century had largely passed this village by. Donkeys plodded through the main street carrying heavy packs on their backs. Food stalls were set up in the little market area. There was the incessant babble of haggling, and people crying out to attract business to their stalls.

I loved to eat the taquitos and the tortillas with the local people in the market area. I would then take the opportunity to share my faith with them. Often I would go from door to door in the village, talking to people about Jesus.

I grew to love the sounds of the swish of brooms as women swept the street in front of their homes, the bell of the garbage collector, and the whistle of the knife sharpener.

I smiled, recalling my own childhood, as I saw shoe-shine boys at work, and youngsters on bicycles with huge, flat baskets of bread balanced on their heads.

On Sunday, I took a succession of services in the mission church. I had thrown myself so much into my new life that I had all but forgotten about the sword of Damocles – my fees – that was hanging over me. The seminary had given me a few odd jobs around the place for which I received some money, and also the mission church paid me a small stipend. That gave me enough to live on, but none was left over for my fees.

I tried to put the problem out of my mind, but then came the day when the three months were up. I was summoned before the faculty staff. They were sitting at a small round table as I was ushered into the room. I could feel a fluttering in my stomach as I stood in front of this august body.

'Peter, won't you sit down?' asked the Dean, drawing up a chair. As I made myself comfortable, he looked decidedly uncomfortable.

Finally his hands stopped their nervous activity and he came straight to the point.

'Peter, we have been discussing your case and we have to ask you if you now have the money to pay for your fees.'

I swallowed.

'I'm afraid not, sir. Nothing has come in yet,' I said, summoning up a smile that I hoped would be convincing.

'Peter,' he said gravely, after an awkward pause. 'We have decided that God has not called you here. You have made a mistake and we want you to leave as soon as possible.'

I looked at him, surprised and dazed.

'But . . .'

'No buts, Peter . . . you must leave.' He shook his head sadly.

I got up wordlessly, a thousand thoughts whirling in my head. Then the full impact of his words became clear. I could stay one more week at the school, then I had to leave.

I felt that I could not just quit my mission church without doing something more to try to reach that village for Christ.

'Lord,' I prayed in my room. 'I don't know what has gone wrong here, but whatever it is I accept it. Please let me serve you in the village for one last time.'

I thought of my friends, The Harvesters, and dashed to their home to tell them the news.

John, one of the quartet, put his huge arm around me and said, 'My dear friend, Peter, just keep trusting the Lord. There is a purpose in all of this. You'll see. The Lord will make it clear.'

I then asked the four of them if they were free on the coming Saturday to sing for me at two final evangelistic meetings at the mission church. Amazingly, they were, and agreed to come.

We handed out invitations in the area, and the members of the church also invited their friends. It was like a fiesta. So many people came that evening that the food sellers set up their stalls outside the building. Many locals stood outside by the sanctuary, licking their ice creams and listening to the amplified proceedings. It was the biggest event to hit the village for a long time.

I felt full of the Holy Spirit at both services and many people came to know the Lord. It was a wonderful moment to be with The Harvesters, just twelve months after my conversion, seeing many others make the same life-changing decision that I had.

That night, back in my dormitory room, it was some time before I restlessly drifted off to sleep. The events of the day had really encouraged me. I felt that God had used me despite the humiliation of having to leave the school. But I still couldn't make sense of being asked to go.

In the darkness, a scenario began to unfurl in my mind. I saw the bearded figure of Moses leading the Israelites away from Egypt and their bondage there. The great man came to the barrier of the Red Sea and complained to God that he had thought He would make things easy for them in the flight to freedom. I distinctly heard the voice of the Lord say to Moses, 'Just go. Don't question me; go forward and I will open up the way for you.'

I woke with a start. It must have been the tacos I had eaten after the crusade services, I thought. They must have affected my digestion. Then I floated off again, and the same story unfolded before me.

This time, however, God turned his attention to me, and said, 'Peter, just go. Don't question what is happening; just go forward and I will open up the way for you!'

With that command still ringing in my ears next morning, I packed my few belongings and slowly walked away from the seminary. No one else was around. The others were all out preaching or attending services. I breathed deeply the mild morning air, then shuffled to the bus station and boarded a bus for Mexico City. I had decided that before returning to Monterrey, I would attend a service in a large church there. Perhaps I would hear a message of hope.

Somehow, though, my mind was in such a whirl that I wasn't very receptive to what the preacher said. I kept wondering how I was going to explain the situation to Blanca and my family.

As I made my way out of the church, someone called my name. I turned in surprise to see Fernando, a distant cousin on my father's side. I was just about to explain my predicament in answer to his friendly enquiry when we were joined by someone else. My cousin introduced me to Aunt Rosita, whom I'd never met before. Before I had got further than explaining how I fitted into the family, she had invited me out for lunch.

'I've heard so much about you,' she said warmly. 'I want you to be my guest.'

I felt embarrassed about my shabby clothes as she ushered me into a huge Oldsmobile that was parked in front of the church. The chauffeur tipped his hat to me.

'Take us to the best restaurant in Mexico City,' she ordered. 'I have a special guest for lunch.'

I had never in all my life ridden in such a vehicle. It cruised noiselessly along the wide city boulevards until we eventually pulled up outside a large restaurant.

Inside, I pored over the huge menu and its high prices. I

felt awkward and self-conscious. 'Sir, I'll have a ham and cheese sandwich,' I told the hovering waiter.

My aunt was horrified.

'Peter, you can have anything on the menu. You are a servant of the Lord. I insist you have the best.' She took the matter into her own hands.

'He'll have prime rib, waiter.'

My eyes nearly popped out of my head when I saw the size of the serving. There was more meat on that plate than I had eaten all month at the seminary.

As we ate, I began to pour out to her the whole story of my conversion, my love for the Lord (and Blanca) and how I had been called to the seminary and then asked to leave.

'Aunt, I don't understand what has happened, but I do know that the Lord has told me that He is going to open up the way for me. I am trusting only in Him.'

Her face showed empathy. She leaned over and clasped my hand.

'Peter, I know we have not met by accident. God has a reason for this.'

After the monster meal, which also included a generous dessert of strawberries and cream, I staggered out of the restaurant into the harsh sunlight.

'Peter, I want you to come and stay the night in my penthouse. I have there what I call the "Prophet's Room". It is reserved only for preachers. I want you to have that room for tonight.'

The pile of the white wall-to-wall carpet in my room seemed four inches thick. The bed was king-sized and was almost as big as my entire room in Monterrey.

I lay back on top of the bed. Then a knock came on the door.

'Peter, I have given my driver a blank cheque and I want you to go with him to the tailor where my late husband used to get his suits. You are to buy whatever you want.'

I was in a daze. Surely, this wasn't happening to me?

When I came back with shirts and trousers and shoes, my aunt shook her head because I had not bought a suit.

'Tomorrow I will take you back myself to have one fitted,

but for now come and hear what I have to say.' She told me that she had been asking God how she could help me.

'I was reading in Matthew, chapter 10.' She pointed to verse 41 and asked me to read it.

'He who receives a prophet because he is a prophet shall receive a prophet's reward, and he who receives a righteous man because he is a righteous man shall receive a righteous man's reward.'

She shut the Bible gently and spoke confidingly to me. 'God has really blessed me and my husband. All I want to do is to share some of that blessing with a prophet – with you. *Esta es tu casa* (my home is yours). Please feel at home.'

For a moment I didn't know what to say.

'I want to take care of all your fees and expenses while you are at seminary. You will never again have to be concerned about money while you are there.' She paused. 'Peter . . .'

I jumped. 'Sorry, Aunt Rosita. I just couldn't believe my ears. You have made me the happiest person alive. Thank you.'

'Don't thank me, thank the Lord. He has provided for you.'

Next evening, I caught the overnight bus to Monterrey, wearing a beautiful pin-striped suit and carrying a new suitcase full of expensive clothes. What a contrast to my first trip to the seminary!

God had confirmed that I should be a minister of the Gospel. The Red Sea had indeed opened up!

9. No More Games

Ruben's jaw dropped open in unfeigned surprise as I walked through the front door of our Monterrey home.

'Wow, Peter, you don't look like a student – more like the owner of the seminary,' he whistled in disbelief.

The family crowded around me. With concern written in her dark eyes, Mother asked, 'Son, what are you doing here? You should be in seminary.'

'They kicked me out, Mama.'

'Why?'

'Because I didn't have any money.'

Rosa, my blonde sister, could contain herself no longer. 'You don't look as if you're about to become a beggar.'

Then Mama turned her delicate face to me. 'Peter, how can you say that you are without money, and yet dress like a king? What happened?'

I told them the whole incredible story. Heads nodded with understanding.

'Are you going back to seminary, then, son?' Mother asked.

'Yes, of course. Aunt Rosita is going to take care of everything.'

I could hardly wait to see Blanca. After her father's untimely death, she had left school, wanting to be company for her mother and also to learn about homemaking. I found her in the front room of her house. Because of the restrictions of our society, we didn't hug or kiss, but our eyes said it all.

'Oh, Chiquita, I have missed you so much,' I told her.

'I've missed you, Peter. I didn't think I would see you for months yet. What is wrong?'

Her face lit up with joy when I told her all that had happened.

'That's wonderful. I knew God had a plan in all of this.' She brushed her long hair away from her dark brown eyes, and smiled.

My pulse was suddenly leaping. She meant so much to me.

'How are you getting on at home?' I asked her.

'Oh, I get so bored. But still, it is good training for when I become a housewife!' Her slightly parted lips gave her a look of expectancy.

'Would you like to become one, then?'

'You know I would.' Blanca's eyes sparkled.

'O.K., let's do it. Let's get married in six months' time.'

'But we have no money, Peter.'

'Don't worry, Chiquita. We belong to a royal family, and God will provide. He has so far.'

*   *   *

It was wonderful to be with my family again, even briefly before I went back to seminary. My brothers and sisters were growing up so fast, and changing so quickly. Only my father and mother were the same, as loving and supportive as ever.

Cesar was now working for a bus-manufacturing company, and for the first time I heard about his union involvement. He had become the youngest-ever union leader at the factory. I was impressed that he should take on such a demanding and even dangerous job.

'What made you do it, Cesar?'

Cesar smiled. 'Peter, I am doing this job as a ministry for Christ. I am doing it to bring justice to the men and women that work at the factory.'

He told me how, over a period of months, he had come to know Christ in a personal way. He had been attending, along with the rest of my family, the church I went to.

'Until I started my union job, I couldn't see any practical application for my faith. But then I saw the terrible cycle that the workers had got themselves into. They would go to work during the week, drink in bars most nights, play soccer on Saturdays, and drink all day Sunday. They were living lives without hope. They had no fight in them to make things better.

'I know that man is made in the image of God and I had to show that to these workers. They had to learn dignity and self-respect. Up until then, most of them had been living purposeless lives.'

So, Cesar explained, he not only began fighting for better conditions and wages for his 1,500 union members, but also shared with them his Christian beliefs.

'I don't know what impact I am having; all I know is that I am doing what I believe God has called me to do.'

Ruben broke into the conversation. 'I too have become aware that our Latin people are being exploited.' He was unusually serious, and his voice was firm with conviction as he told me he was going to become a lawyer. He felt sure that was the best way he could help. My heart thrilled as I realised that I was not the only member of my family who was finding a real purpose in life.

We were a family who loved to sit around and talk. The new radio my father had acquired was hardly ever on. Talking was our greatest pleasure, and on this occasion particularly there was so much news to catch up on that we chatted for hours.

Nellie, our eldest sister, brewed several pots of tea to help the flow of conversation. She had recently become the official secretary to the church, and Mama whispered to me that Rosa had just started working in the technical section of a radio station.

'Rosa is especially happy because she now has some money,' added my mother. 'She hates being poor.'

I felt increasingly proud of my family. We were indeed the royal family my mother had impressed upon us. What might the younger ones do eventually? I looked affectionately at Olivia, aged eleven; Maria, eight; and Ricardo, now five years old. I felt sad that I had to leave them all again to go back to the seminary.

*   *   *

The registrar showed no surprise as I walked through the door of the seminary on my return.

'It's good to have you back,' he greeted me warmly. 'We received a cheque from your aunt and we are happy to welcome you again. You can move back to your same dormitory room.'

I looked at him in surprise. I suppose I expected an apology. 'May I ask you a question, sir?'

'Sure. Fire away.'

'Do you think that maybe God did want me here after all?'

He looked at me, obviously wondering what lay behind my question. Then he cleared his throat and said, 'Are you asking if we made a mistake in asking you to leave, Peter?'

I nodded, a mischievous grin playing about my face.

'I don't know. All I know is that the Bible says that "all things do work together for good to those that love God". So whatever the rights and wrongs of this situation, God had a purpose in it.'

The other students gasped as I entered the dormitory. Suddenly I was the best-dressed student in the place. I had new confidence.

As time went on, however, my self-assurance began to get the better of me. I didn't notice how arrogant I was becoming. I would argue with the professors over the minutest things. I would complain about the food we were given, the living conditions, the curriculum. Then I would look to the rest of the students for recognition and admiration of my daring.

One day I was called before the faculty. The Dean looked severe.

'You have really disappointed us, Peter. We thought you were a better Christian than this.'

'What do you mean?' I was outraged. 'You mean that you are not prepared to even listen to my legitimate complaints. You are not for justice!'

'Now, Peter, we are not saying that.'

'Well, what are you saying?'

This confrontation was repeated several more times. I took a perverse pleasure in speaking my mind. I suppose I thought back to Cesar fighting for his union members in the factory, and felt I had to assume a similar role at the seminary.

But it wasn't all sad. I had taken over again as pastor of the mission church in Zacatelco, and one Saturday I invited a couple of the students to join me in some visitation work in an even smaller nearby village.

'Stick with me and I'll show you how it's done,' I told Luis and Ramiro, my companions.

I knocked on a few doors with my friends looking on and went through my you-need-to-get-saved routine, like a salesman. I offered each person a Gospel of John.

'O.K., let's split up and you take a house each.'

They had learned quickly and soon were following my 'script'. We were so intent on what we were doing that none of us noticed a menacing crowd of youths assembling a short distance away. It was only when sharp stones were thrown at our legs that we were alerted to the danger. 'Hey, you Hallelujahs,' shouted the leader, using an insulting expression for Protestants. 'Get out of here. This is a Catholic town. We don't want heretics here.'

My two companions looked at me for a response, but before I could say anything three of the thugs made a grab for Luis. I caught the look of horror on his face.

'Leave him alone,' I yelled furiously. 'He's not done anything to you. All we want to give you is the Word of God.' My mind began working feverishly, looking for some way out. They had the advantage over us, being so many, and before we knew it we were being dragged over to a large tree. Rope was produced and red, calloused hands tied us up. I twisted my face to the side and desperately tried to struggle free but the rope was too strong and burned my wrists.

'We're going to kill you. Prepare to die.'

I saw the glint of machetes in the sunlight. At that moment I found myself praying involuntarily.

'Lord, if you want me to die, I'm ready. But before I do, I want to apologise for my behaviour over the past months. I didn't take your calling seriously.'

Tears began running down my cheeks. Not because I was about to die, but for the blindness of this killer mob. Love for them surprisingly flowed from inside me.

I could imagine how Jesus must have felt on the cross, blameless, yet being killed. Despite his complete innocence, He asked for forgiveness for his executors. In contrast, I was guilty (not least of arrogant behaviour), and deserved punishment.

'Stop! Stop! Don't do anything.' A new voice broke into my terror and my prayers. I opened my eyes and saw a middle-aged man in a khaki uniform. He was a member of the rural police, and he had two women with him who seemed vaguely familiar.

I suddenly recognised them: we'd given them Gospels. They must have alerted the policeman.

The group began to back off as the policeman threatened to call the soldiers. The leader smiled bitterly. Finally they all shuffled away, and we were untied. As we straightened our clothing, our rescuer told us to get out of town immediately.

'Don't come back, because if you do I can't guarantee your safety. That was a very foolish thing you did.'

'But what's wrong with giving out the Word of God? That's all we were doing.' I was perplexed.

'I know, but this town is Catholic. Just leave it as it is.'

We trudged towards the main road, where we hoped to pick up a bus back to Zacatelco. My heart was full of thanks to God. I prayed silently.

'Lord, you have made me realise that I have just been playing games recently, trying to be clever and attract attention to myself. Never again do I want to do that. From now on, I am going to be deadly serious for you. I am going to serve you until the end of my days.'

10. 'For Better, for Worse'

'. . . For better, for worse . . . I now declare you man and wife.'

Blanca looked so beautiful in her silk wedding dress. Through her veil I saw a look of happiness that melted my heart. We squeezed hands and then turned around and slowly began walking down the aisle to Mendelssohn's 'Wedding March'.

It had been a day to remember. We had already gone through *por el civil*, a civil marriage, which is compulsory by Mexican law. Now came *por la iglesia*, the church marriage. Our church in Monterrey was packed to capacity. My mother and father looked so smart in their newly made wedding outfits. My brothers and sisters also looked immaculate.

The wedding reception took place in a local social club. It was lots of fun with plenty of games to enjoy, like pass-the-parcel. Blanca and I joined in with gusto. When the time came for the meal, Blanca couldn't eat because she was so excited. So, after I had wolfed down my chicken salad, I looked at Blanca, and said, 'My wife, I have an important request.'

'Yes, Peter, what is it?'

'Can I have your dinner? It seems a shame to waste it . . .'

It was midnight when all the festivities had finally come to an end. My sister Nellie could see how excited we were, so she made a suggestion to help us unwind.

'Let me take you in my car to the top of Obispado, and

you can sit there and watch the lights of the city for a while.'

When we arrived at the top of the hill, Nellie suggested I go off to a quiet spot and just sit and talk with my new wife.

As we watched the blinking, flickering lights illuminating the valley below, we both began crying.

'Lord,' I wept, 'I can't believe that finally you have brought us together in marriage. I am so happy that I am going to spend the rest of my life with Blanca.'

She wiped away her tears, and continued: 'Lord, we want this to be a Christian marriage. We want to serve you together.'

I touched the back of Blanca's neck lightly. Then I turned and kissed her. At last we were married and there was no fear of a chaperone intervening, or reporting us. We both felt intensely alive.

When we got back to the car I asked Nellie if she would take us to Mario's home to pick up our suitcases, so we could catch the early morning bus to a nearby town, where we planned to spend the first three days of our married life. Then we were to go to Juarez, which was 600 miles away, where I had been invited to become the pastor of a church for the next three months.

We held hands in the car, and after twenty minutes arrived at her brother Mario's.

I greeted him happily on the front porch.

'Mario, hi, how are you?'

He didn't respond. He looked at Blanca, his face as black as thunder.

'Where have you been, Blanca?' His words trembled with anger. 'I have been waiting here since the party. Why didn't you come straight home?'

'But Mario,' she said, taken aback, 'I have been with my husband.'

'I don't want excuses, you should have been home ages ago,' he shouted. 'Get inside!'

'But Mario, I am going on my honeymoon . . .' The words died in her throat.

'Don't argue, sister. Go inside and go straight to bed.' We looked at each other, frankly disbelieving. He ushered

Blanca through the door with a flourish of his arm and followed her inside. As he slammed the door behind him I stood aghast. The shock of what had happened left me speechless. I stood, blinking for a moment, trying to take in the situation.

Having seen his volatile temper I decided not to argue with Mario, but to go back to my family. At least I could get a good sleep and they I would try to rescue my bride in the morning.

Mama sleepily opened the front door. She looked at me in surprise as I stood there, acutely embarrassed.

'Son, what are you doing here?'

'Mama, Mario won't let me and Blanca be together tonight. I thought I would come and spend the night here and then get her tomorrow.'

'But,' she said, 'we have no room for you. You know our relatives have travelled a long way to be at your wedding. Now they are sleeping all over the house.'

'But what can I do, Mama?' This marriage-night was turning into a nightmare.

'Well, the only place where there is room is the patio. You could curl up there. Why don't you roll up your jacket and use that as a pillow?'

I did!

Next day, I convinced Mario that my intentions were honourable, and Blanca and I were finally allowed to depart for our honeymoon.

*   *   *

We had three blissful months away, first on our honeymoon, and then in the temporary pastorate. We spent many wonderful hours together, learning more and more about each other. I enjoyed being able to share what God was teaching me from the Bible with Blanca, and also with the congregation in Juarez.

Then came the time for me to return to seminary. We travelled to Puebla together and managed to rent a small room near the school.

Aunt Rosita, as always, was faithful in paying my fees and also sending me some spending money. But now I had to support a wife as well as myself.

'We will never be able to live on the money that my aunt sends me,' I told Blanca one day. 'I will have to try to get a job to supplement the money.'

'Maybe I could look for a job,' she said gently.

I was angry. 'Blanca, if I cannot support you myself, I should not have married. Please put that thought out of your head.'

We knelt down and prayed, asking the Lord that if it was His will to get me work so that I could supplement the money Aunt Rosita sent me.

Shortly afterwards, I was sharing my need for a job with members of The Harvesters, and one of them, Samuel, said, 'Peter, do you know José Hernandez? He is the director of the local newspaper here.'

Blanca cut in, 'I know José. He's my cousin's husband. I didn't know he was living in Puebla.'

So we went to see José and his wife Elvita. They welcomed us with open arms. After much warm hugging and laughing, we were offered coffee.

As we sat and exchanged news with this lovely Christian couple, José turned his attention to me.

'Hey, Peter, if you ever want a job, I could use you on the newspaper.'

'That's wonderful, José. We have been praying that the Lord would provide work to help us survive here.'

'Well, the Lord has heard your prayer!'

So, each night, after my studies, I would head for the busy offices of the daily newspaper, and work as a switch-board operator.

I was soon completely absorbed in my busy life. I would have to be at the seminary at seven-thirty a.m. for classes, which ended at one o'clock. After a lunch break, I would rehearse for an hour with the seminary's singing quartet of which I was now a member. Then I would get on my bicycle and pedal furiously to reach the newspaper offices by three-thirty p.m. I worked there until midnight and then I would stagger home happy, but tired, at twelve-thirty a.m. Usually, by then, Blanca was fast asleep.

One night, after four months, I literally fell into bed, hardly able to think straight after another hectic, but fulfilling, day. But on this occasion Blanca was wide awake. She was sitting up in bed, crying softly and reading her Bible. Her face was strained and pale, and tears were running down her cheeks.

'What's the matter, Chiquita?' I was shocked.

She turned her sad dark eyes on mine.

'Peter, I don't think you love me any more.' Her lower lip quivered with emotion.

'That's not true. Why do you say that?'

'Because you're never with me any more. I feel so lonely being here all the time. I didn't think marriage would be like this. I thought we would be together all the time.'

It was then that I realised how selfish I had been. I was enjoying every moment of my new life: the Bible studies, the fellowship with the students and staff, the singing, and even my job. But poor Blanca was confined to four walls as my dutiful wife. And I was selfishly expecting her to find fulfilment with that. I suddenly felt her pain and anguish.

'Let's do something about this, Blanca.'

'But what?' Her hazel eyes burned into mine.

'Why don't you start attending some of the classes with me at the seminary?'

'I'd love to.'

'And . . .' I searched my mind for something more. 'You could bring my dinner to the newspaper on the bus, so we can spend my break together.'

She smiled, relaxing at last.

'Peter, thank you. But, please, don't let us ever stop talking to each other because one or the other becomes too busy. Marriage has to be a two-way sharing of everything.'

I held Blanca in my arms and kissed away her tears.

'Forgive me, Chiquita.'

My job at the newspaper was just for weekdays, so that left the weekend free for me to be involved in evangelistic outreach to the towns and villages around Puebla as well as in the city itself. Despite what had happened on my last attempt to preach the Gospel in a new town, I was convinced that God had called me to share my faith with the people of my country.

One evening, I was sitting up in bed, my Bible open, reviewing the sermon I was due to deliver that Saturday night, when suddenly I felt a bump on the bed. What was happening? Suddenly a pressure came as if a hand were pressing against my mouth and nose, trying to suffocate me. I cried out to Blanca, but she didn't seem to hear. She began moaning in her sleep. Then a cold, invisible hand pressed down on my chest. I gasped for breath; then my arms went completely stiff, as if they were pinned by my side. I tried to pull my arm over to wake my wife, but the stiffness made it impossible.

'Oh, my God,' I choked. 'Please help me.'

I felt myself almost sinking out of consciousness, but managed to cry out, 'I rebuke you, Satan's spirit.' My heart ran wildly, my pulse thudded. 'Jesus has power over you. Leave me.'

Blanca was still moaning, but didn't awake. This terrifying battle went on for nearly thirty minutes. Then, suddenly, I felt the pressure ease and the strange force went away.

I lay back on the pillow shaking with fright. It was the most scaring experience of my life.

'Oh God, thank you for saving my life. I don't understand what was happening there, but I know that was not of you.'

All night long I drifted between consciousness and unconsciousness. Several times I awoke with a start. My mouth was soured with the taste of fear.

Next day, I shared the experience with Elpidio, one of the students I had grown close to. He was a Mixteco Indian from Oaxaca, in the south of Mexico.

He listened gravely to my description of what had occurred in my bedroom.

'Do you think I am going crazy or something?' I finished. I was wondering if all the hard work had warped my mind a little. He caught the tone of hysteria in my voice.

'No,' he said firmly, 'not at all. Nor do I think that you imagined what happened last night.'

He opened his Bible and found Ephesians 6:12. He began reading, 'For we are not contending against flesh and blood, but against the principalities, against the powers, against the world rulers of this present darkness, against the spiritual hosts of wickedness in the heavenly places.'

A similar attack occurred six months later. I was preparing for a weekend crusade when an unseen but very real hand tried to suffocate me.

This time I knew who he was and I claimed the protection of the blood of Jesus. The battle was again terrifying, but I knew this time that I would be victorious. I also knew that the crusade was going to be a success. As Blanca again lay asleep but moaning, as if in pain, the evil spirit finally left.

I knew that Jesus had helped me win this spiritual battle. But I was also aware that there would be many more to come, as I invaded Satan's territory in Latin America.

11. On the Road Again

The telegram boy knocked urgently at the front door of my parents' home. I peered through the window and saw the slight figure of a teenager, anxiously fingering the message. He was still trying to catch his breath after pedalling from the post office on his bicycle.

My mother went to the door and I heard the messenger say, 'It's for Mr. Peter Asael Gonzalez. It's very urgent.' What could have happened? After two more years, I had finally graduated from seminary. We had stayed on in Puebla for about nine months afterwards so that I could help establish a Christian bookshop, supported by the seminary.

During that time our first child, Nellie, a bouncing daughter, was born. She was the image of her mother. Now we were back with my parents for a short break.

My mother handed me the telegram.

'I do hope it isn't trouble,' she said.

I was apprehensive. Who would send this to me? What could be the problem?

I ripped it open anxiously and scanned the message. It read, 'Peter, I offer you the post of representative for the Bible Society of Mexico. Signed José Hernandez.'

'Isn't that my cousin's husband?' asked Blanca, who was by now peering over my shoulder. 'I thought he was still with the newspaper.'

'Yes, it is. Perhaps he has left. I wonder what this means.' I was pleased with the message. Then I spotted, out of the corner of my eye, the young telegram boy still standing there, coughing pointedly.

'Oh, I'm sorry.' I handed him a peso and he saluted me.

I looked at Blanca. 'What do you think, Chiquita?'

'It sounds exciting. Why don't you go to Mexico City and see what it is all about?'

I sent a message back to José saying that I would see him the following week.

* * *

When I arrived at his home, it was already late evening. He seemed delighted to see me.

As his wife provided me with delicious enchiladas, topped with lashings of hot melted cheese, he began talking.

'I left my job on the paper when I was asked if I would help reorganise the work of the Bible Society of Mexico,' he explained.

'We are setting up a training programme for churches all over the country so that their members can use the Scriptures to evangelise their areas. We want you to be one of the people to train them. You'll travel for a month with the general manager and another representative. That will be your training.'

Next morning, José took me into the Bible Society office in Mexico City, and introduced me to Daniel Lopez, the general manager. He was extremely friendly and outlined the job I was being offered. After just a few minutes, he could see that I was already hooked.

'I'll pay you 1,000 pesos (£40) a month,' he informed me.

I asked for a few moments to collect my thoughts. The job sounded all I had ever wanted. But I didn't want to accept just because I felt good about it. I wanted the Lord to confirm it to me.

He suggested that I walk around the block to think a little and then come back with my answer. So I went out into the streets, busy as usual with crawling traffic. As I walked with the milling crowds of people, the stinging pollution trapped under the clouds hurt my lungs.

I prayed as I walked. 'Lord, I don't want to be irreverent, but I would definitely like to know from you what I should do. I would like to follow the example of Gideon and put out another fleece. God, do you want to use me to help deliver my people from being ignorant of your Scriptures? Please give me a sign!'

I went back to see Mr. Lopez.

'O.K., Peter, what is your verdict?'

I told him of the fleece I had put out to the Lord. 'I will not accept one centavo from you for a month. If I fail in my job, I will then go back to Monterrey and all I will ask of you is my bus fare. But if you are happy with what I am doing, I want you to pay me 1,200 pesos (£50) a month. That is the total income I was getting from the newspaper and my aunt when I was living in Puebla.'

He looked at me dumbfounded. Then he broke into a chuckle.

'Brother Peter, that is wonderful. Many people place a fleece like this before the Lord, but they already have their own answers worked out in their minds. But you are doing something really practical. Something that may cost you a lot of money. I accept your proposition.'

I called Blanca at her family home and told her of my bargain with God. There was a pause on the other end of the line. Then she responded:

'Peter, you know we desperately need money at this time, especially now we have our baby, but I agree, we must walk with the Lord. Please go ahead with what you have agreed with the Bible Society.'

I was delighted with her reaction, and told her that I was immediately setting off on a trip with the two Bible Society men. I asked her to join me part of the way through the journey in Tampico.

Our first stop was to be a big test of my faith. It was at a church belonging to a denomination which, I had been told by people at my own church in Monterrey, was heretical.

'Only our denomination has the real truth,' one leader there had told me.

That fallacy had been partly shaken during my time at

the interdenominational seminary. But I had not before been exposed to this particular group. I arrived in quite an aggressive mood, fully prepared to be the defender of the truth among them.

On the first day, the church was packed with wide-eyed young men and women, all wanting to drink in every word of the seminar. I was happy with their enthusiasm and love for the Word of God.

'Peter,' said Mr. Lopez, 'I want you to go out door-to-door this afternoon with the assistant pastor. That will be a good experience for you.'

But, I thought, he is one of the men leading this flock into a wrong theology. Maybe I should tackle him on this as we do our rounds.

'Brother,' I asked as we walked to the block where we were to start our outreach, 'can I ask you what you believe about salvation?'

He seemed surprised. But still he graciously showed me from the Scriptures his beliefs. They tallied exactly with mine. I then pressed him for his theology on a range of subjects and was again amazed that they almost completely tied in with mine. It was at that moment I fully understood a passage I'd read earlier in Acts that had never been clear to me: Acts 10:15. 'And the voice came to him a second time, "What God has cleansed, you must not call common." '

That was what God told Peter when his tradition told him that certain things were unclean. I realised now that I had no right to consider other denominations 'unclean'. That was if we both had the same head: Jesus.

The trip was a great success. I enjoyed working closely with so many new people and learning that God was not confined to a tiny denominational box, but was working all over His Church. I was also able to confess to the assistant pastor my earlier misgivings, assuring him that I now understood as never before that we were all part of the same body. Blanca joined me for part of the journey and then I went back to the Mexico City office of the Bible Society to await the verdict. She took our baby to Puebla to stay temporarily with Elvita, the wife of José Hernandez.

I spent the next five days writing reports and wondering what God's answer was going to be. I was deeply engrossed in the litter of paperwork on my desk when the phone rang. It was Mr. Lopez, inviting me to his office.

My hands lingered on the receiver for a moment, then I headed nervously for his office. I rapped on the door once, and walked in.

'Sit down, Peter, I have an answer for you.' His eyes were fixed on my face.

'The fleece is dry,' he said firmly, 'but the ground is wet.'

My mind went blank. What was he talking about?

'Don't you remember the fleece that Gideon put forth?'

'Of course!' I could have kicked myself.

He then stretched out his hand and handed me an envelope.

'Open it, Peter.'

It contained a cheque from the Bible Society of Mexico for 1,200 pesos.

'You're on, Peter. You are part of the team.' I rose to my feet, trembling slightly. The vigil of waiting was over.

* * *

The white-haired old lady was gently rocking in her chair on the porch of a modest adobe, red-tile-roofed house in a town in the south of Mexico, when I called on her. I could see through an open door that she had a brick floor. I also noted that she had a makeshift altar in the main room of the house. This was placed on a table on which were candles, flowers, incense burners and a large image of Mary.

'Which Bible are you selling, sir? The Catholic or the Protestant one?'

It was early evening and a fly was buzzing around my ear.

'It's just the Bible, ma'am.'

'Yes, young man.' She leaned forward and I saw the net of wrinkles around her eyes. She was certainly from old-time Mexico. 'But there are two Bibles, aren't there?'

'No, madam, there is only one Bible. God spoke only once and Jesus, our Saviour, lived just once.'

Her eyes were now wide open with frank curiosity.

I showed her two different versions of the Bible that I had with me, and compared John 3:16.

'You see, the meaning is the same. They just say it in a slightly different way so that people can understand more fully.'

I could see her interest increase. She examined one version that contained beautiful pictures to illustrate some of the stories.

'O.K., young man. You seem very sincere, especially for a Protestant. I'll buy a copy of the illustrated Bible.'

Before I left I wrote down some key verses for her to read, and thanked her for her purchase.

My companion on this occasion was Miguel, a young believer from a local church. He had come along with me for training, and was already moved to discover so much ignorance among his people about the Bible.

As we came to the next porch, where a burly middle-aged man was sitting, I watched Miguel swallow deeply. It was his turn to carry the conversation. The man's sombrero was pushed down over his eyes, and a cigarette dangled on his lower lip.

'Yes . . . what do you want?' Miguel literally jumped at the sharp sound of his voice. The man took a swig from a bottle of beer.

'I've come to share with you . . .' My companion's voice was trembling.

I began to pray for Miguel as he put into practice what he had learned from the seminar I had conducted, and was glad to see that he'd already taken in a great deal. He was smartly dressed. Earlier that day, I had spoken angrily to the young people who had come sloppily dressed for the door-to-door work. One teenage girl turned up wearing a flimsy beach dress and sandals. Her hair was up, as though she were going for a swim.

I'd told her to go home and change. 'You are about to represent God's Holy Word, and you should give a good impression. If someone sees you like that they will think what you have for them is not worth much.'

The more I handled and read the Word of God, the more I grew to love and respect it. I knew that it was not something to be taken lightly. It was holy; it had to be treated with reverence.

I told the young people we were training that I wanted them to go back again one week later to people who had bought a Bible, to encourage them to continue to read the Scriptures and to help them with it.

'For five weeks I want you to visit them,' I emphasised. 'You will become a friend; then, after that time, I want you to organise a little Bible study in a house in that *barrio* and invite people along to a simple study in a home.'

I suggested some themes: how to be saved (Mark 1:40–45); the love of God (Luke 15:11–32); the grace of God (Mark 10:46–52); and the forgiveness of sin (John 4:1–42).

'It is best to develop these themes through questions and answers,' I explained, assuring them at the same time that we were not the first to do this. I asked them to turn with me to Acts 15:36. 'And after some days Paul said to Barnabas, "Come, let us return and visit the brethren in every city where we proclaimed the Word of the Lord and see how they are." '

I added: 'We are only following these principles. I want you to continue these Bible groups for several more weeks. Why? Because, when you come to the point of asking them to accept Christ as their personal Saviour, they will know what you are talking about. That is most important. They will see that these are not just your words and ideas, but they come from God Himself in the Holy Scriptures.'

I then flicked my Bible to Isaiah 55:11, reading aloud, 'So shall my word be that goes forth from my mouth; it shall not return to me empty, but it shall accomplish that which I purpose, and prosper in the thing for which I sent it.'

'Remember those words,' I concluded, 'and claim that promise.'

*   *   *

I was delighted to see Cesar again at our little flat in Mexico

City. He had arrived earlier in the day and I gave him a warm *abrazo*, as I entered the living room.

'Cesar, it is good to see you.' I told him of my latest trip and all that had happened.

'But, Peter, you look very tired,' Cesar interrupted. It was true: month after month of travel was taking its toll. Each glance in the mirror confirmed to me that all was not well.

'I have some news that may help you pep up a little,' continued my brother warmly. 'Grandfather Emilio is setting up an engineering workshop in Monterrey and he wants us to run it for him. I wondered if you would like the idea.'

The proposition took me by surprise. I had initially felt I was to be with the Bible Society for life. But here, all of a sudden, was an alternative.

I looked at Blanca, and rubbed my chin. She looked away.

'Chiquita, that would mean we could be together much more,' I told her. 'I wouldn't have to travel all over the country as I do now. And . . .' I finished with a confession. 'I am feeling a little stale after three years with the Bible Society.'

Looking around our sparsely-furnished flat, I knew we also needed some extra money. 'Perhaps God is telling us that He wants us back in Monterrey, to serve Him there,' I pleaded, searching for assurance from Blanca. 'Perhaps this is a good time for me to start making some real money.'

I saw a brief flash of panic on her face. Then one single tear ran silently down her cheek.

12. An Act of Treason

'But you promised that we would spend some time this morning on Bible reading and prayer.' There was despair and pain in Blanca's voice.

I grabbed my dirty overalls and began climbing into them.

'Look, Chiquita, I can't stop now. We have a big order coming in for car parts. We have a deadline to finish them. Maybe tomorrow . . .'

'But you said that yesterday . . . and the day before.'

Why did Blanca keep on at me? Couldn't she see that I was trying to provide a better way of life for her and our two children, Nellie and Azael?

'Look,' I sighed impatiently. 'I'm not going to argue. Cesar is waiting for me at the workshop. See you tonight. I don't know what time I will be in.' But I felt bad at having spoken to Blanca in such a curt way.

My step to the workshop that Monday morning was slow. This was just four months after I had left the Bible Society to become a 'rich industrialist'. I had sincerely thought it was right for me to get involved in this project. Surely soon we would be reaping the benefit.

'Did you go to church last night?' asked Cesar as I arrived.

'I'm afraid not, brother. I was just too tired.' It was a lame excuse.

'You haven't been for some time now, have you?'

He was getting at me just like Blanca.

That day my sense of guilt was wrapped around me like a

chain, and nothing seemed to ease its stranglehold. I kept thinking, 'What am I doing in this smelly building, doing work I don't enjoy one little bit?'

I was existing in the midst of a nightmare. I knew beyond doubt that Blanca was unhappy too, so what was the point of it?

That night, with tiredness coursing through me, I stumbled into the living room of our home. I just fell on to the couch. I had a blinding headache. Blanca came and sat next to me. I could see she wanted to say something, but didn't quite know how to start. I realised that I had isolated her from myself. So I took a deep breath and tried to take charge of the situation.

'O.K., Chiquita, I know what you want to say.' She looked away in embarrassment. She hated confrontations, knowing that by now my temper burned on a short fuse.

'You are going to tell me I've made a mistake,' I snapped.

She didn't answer.

'Well, you're right.' Blanca still said nothing. 'I made a terrible mistake. Chiquita, I am the most miserable man alive.' My voice faltered. 'I have committed an act . . . of treason. I have left God's royal way.'

Blanca tenderly snuggled closer.

'Chiquita, let's pray right now.'

I lay back on the couch and opened my heart to God. 'Lord,' I cried, 'please forgive me. I thought that money would be everything, but now I know it isn't. I want to start serving you again and do only your will . . .'

With that, deep sobs shook me. It was as if I were allowing God to wash away all remembrance of those terrible four months.

'Don't cry, Peter.' Blanca knelt down beside me and began kissing away my tears. 'God never did leave you. He was just waiting for you to come to this place so He could forgive you. Now let's ask Him to show us what we should do.'

A new lightness and resilience came into my step as I walked to the workshop next morning. The husky figures of

Grandfather Emilio and Cesar were waiting for me. Both were smiling.

'Hi, Peter, I have some good news for you.'

'Yes, Grandpa, what is it?'

'We've had a really big order in today. It will keep you busy for months.'

I grimaced with acute embarrassment.

'Before you go any further,' I interjected, 'I have something to tell you and Cesar.' This was the moment to be honest. The pair looked puzzled, so I didn't prolong the agony.

'I'm sorry, but I'm going to leave.' They stared awkwardly, then Cesar reacted.

'You what? But the business is just getting on its feet.'

I determined not to weaken.

'All I know is that I made a mistake. I have told God that I want to go back into the ministry.'

Both shook their heads and looked at each other. I felt I owed them a further explanation.

'I was reading this morning in 2 Timothy 2:4: "No soldier on service gets entangled in civilian pursuits, since his aim is to satisfy the one who enlisted him." By taking this job, I deserted from the Lord's Army. Now I'm going to enlist again . . . for good!'

With that I shook hands with them both, gathered up my belongings and left.

Soon afterwards, I received a phone call from José Hernandez. He was still at the Bible Society, and told me that someone from the Latin America Mission had been trying to contact me.

'Apparently,' he explained, 'one of their missionaries from the United States is arriving at Monterrey Airport in a couple of days and he wants to see you.'

Me? I was intrigued. At the required time, I was waiting at the barrier.

'Lord, I haven't a clue what this man looks like. Please show me.'

Someone tapped my shoulder, and I turned to confront a man with a long, lean and weather-beaten face. He wore a light brown sports jacket, an open-necked shirt and grey trousers.

'I'm Hal Carter from the Latin America Mission.' I shook his hand warmly, and introduced myself. I still didn't really understand why I was there.

Once he was safely installed in his hotel, I prepared to leave.

'Mr. Carter, if I can be of further service, please contact me. I'd be happy to drive you anywhere you want while you are here. I have just resigned from my job so I have plenty of free time.'

'Hey, don't leave, Peter. Didn't you get the message about why I wanted to see you?'

'No . . .'

He asked me to sit down.

'Brother Peter, I help run Editorial Caribe, the publishing arm of our mission. We are planning to open a branch here in Mexico. We think you could be just the man to run it.'

My first instinct was to laugh.

'But,' I spluttered, 'I thought I was just here to be your chauffeur!'

He gave a relaxed smile. 'Peter, what on earth gave you that idea? My brother, I have come to offer you the job. You may be a good driver, but I wouldn't fly from Costa Rica to see if you could handle a car or not. What do you say, then?'

'But why me?' I was perplexed.

Mr. Carter explained that I had been highly recommended by the Bible Society.

'But I don't deserve such a job . . .'

'What was that, Peter?'

'Oh, nothing.'

When he was settled in, I took him to a restaurant that specialised in goat-meat steaks. There he outlined in more detail the job he wanted me to do. My heart pounded with excitement.

'Peter, will you come to see me with your wife tomorrow, and give me your decision?'

'Of course, Mr. Carter.'

Blanca had been waiting up for me.

'Peter, you look happy. What happened?'

'You will never guess what I have been asked to do . . .'

*   *   *

For three months I spent a few days in each department of Editorial Caribe learning about its operation.

'We want our publications in Mexico,' explained Mr. Carter. 'We feel there is a great need there for Christian books, concordances, and especially the Gospel Light Sunday School materials.'

After our short stay in San José, we moved to bustling Mexico City and I opened our new office. It was housed in the Bible Society building, which was an added bonus for me, as I was able to meet many of my old friends again. Soon we built up our stocks of Christian literature, and I was able to begin touring Mexico, making many contacts with churches and bookshops.

I threw myself, heart and soul, into the ministry. I was so happy to be back doing the Lord's work. One rain-soaked evening, I was on the way to Tampico with Blanca's brother Mario, who had come along to keep me company. By now we were firm friends. My car was packed full with literature for a Christian booksellers' convention. We were in high spirits and had spent much of the journey singing hymns and choruses at the tops of our voices.

I had completed three-quarters of the four-hundred-mile journey when rain began tumbling down thickly out of the darkness of the evening sky. I slowed down a little, but I didn't want to cut back my speed too much; we needed to be in Tampico in good time to get some sleep before setting up the display early the following morning.

Suddenly Mario gasped and grabbed my arm.

'Look out, Peter!'

A huge bus was careering towards us, its headlights full on. I was blinded. The windscreen wipers clicked back and forth in a hopeless struggle to clear away the torrent of rain, as I swerved desperately to avoid the bus. I slammed on the brakes. Everything seemed to be happening in slow motion, and the car began to skid.

Suddenly I felt the car leave the road. We rolled over and over down the embankment and into the creek below, where we came to a grinding halt. A huge fallen tree barred our way. There, just inches ahead, was a large lake. Our headlights shone into the choppy waters: we had been heading straight for it.

'Are you all right, Mario?'

'I think so.' He was breathing heavily, and his face was spattered with blood. Flying glass from the windscreen had hit us both, but thankfully there were no broken limbs.

The car had come to rest at a crazy angle, almost completely on its side. Mario managed to unwind his window and slowly clambered out. Then I followed him. I noticed that much of our literature had been thrown out onto the wet ground.

There was a buzz of concerned chatter on the road above.

'Are you people down there O.K.?' one voice shouted.

'I think so. But the car's stuck,' I yelled back.

Soon several villagers slithered down to us, and with their help the car was set on its wheels again. Meanwhile, the bus driver had ignored the situation completely, and thundered on through the night towards Mexico City.

I fumbled with the ignition. At first nothing happened, but the second time the engine caught. The fallen tree was heaved out of the way, and slowly we eased the crippled vehicle back onto the road.

I couldn't thank the villagers enough.

'Please, I must give you something.'

They all shook their heads.

'No, go quickly. *And may God be with you*!'

I shook hands with them through the window; as I drove away, their words rang in my ears.

Although I was doing so much travelling, I usually forgot to ask the Lord to be with me. I was right back in the thick of the spiritual battle and yet I knew that I was often fighting with my weapons, instead of God's.

'Let's just pull over to the side of the road and pray,' I said to Mario, realising for the first time how near we had been to death.

'Lord, I'm sorry for the crazy way I've been driving, and also for forgetting to commit this and other journeys into your hands. In the future, I will not travel without inviting you to be beside me.'

I managed to get some temporary repairs done to the car in Tampico, and after the booksellers' convention, I headed on to the next stop on my itinerary, Monterrey. The car limped along at thirty miles an hour and I had to drive peering through a hole in the shattered windscreen.

'Mario, do you know something?' I said to my companion. 'I need some help. I believe I should look around for other people to help share the load of this new job.'

Then it came to me. 'What about Cesar? Maybe he could join me.'

Mario agreed. 'I heard the workshop isn't going too well. Cesar is feeling the pressure, and he isn't making the big profits he had hoped for.'

I put the car into a garage in Monterrey to be fixed properly, and then went to see my brother. He saw me at the entrance and came over, grinning and wiping the oil from his hands. Streaks of sweat covered his face.

As he put down the soiled towel, I hugged him.

'Hey, my brother, I have a proposition to put to you.'

He raised his eyebrows questioningly.

'How would you like to have your hands clean – for *ever*?' I chuckled.

13. 'Suffer the Little Thieves . . .'

The crowds streamed out of Arena Mexico in Mexico City. We were all in good spirits as my country had just crushed Puerto Rico in an exciting international basketball game.

'Let's go and eat some tortas,' I suggested to Cesar and José Becktol, a Peruvian-born friend who was working with Editorial Caribe in Costa Rica. José was enroute to San José from the United States and had stopped off to see us both.

The nearby restaurant was packed with happy Mexicans, proud that we had scored such a decisive victory over our Latin rivals. When we finally were shown to a table, José began inquiring about our family.

When he asked about Ruben, I became serious.

'I'm worried about him,' I confessed. 'He is one of the leaders of a leftist student group at the university. They are mixed up in a lot of disturbances these days.' The students were becoming very active, and I was afraid that Ruben, as a leader in their protests, might get hurt. Our government took a hard line on such behaviour.

José changed the subject, trying to dispel the gloom that was threatening to spoil our afternoon. He and Cesar began a lively conversation.

'So, do you plan to stay at the office?'

The question came as a surprise, since Cesar had only been working with me for six months. He was enjoying the work and doing well.

'Why do you ask?' Cesar replied. José finished his chicken tortas, and leaned back in his seat.

'Well . . .' he said slowly, as if preparing us for something important. 'You are a man of potential, Cesar, and I want to ask if you would be interested in coming to Costa Rica to attend the Latin America Mission seminary there?' Cesar looked at him in astonishment. 'I would pay for all your travel costs and also take care of your fees,' José finished.

This was a completely new idea for Cesar. He hadn't considered going to seminary. For a moment he said nothing and busied himself with ordering some *cajeta*, a caramelised goat's milk that looks and tastes like butterscotch sauce.

'This will help me think better,' he explained, not too convincingly.

That night, I could hear Cesar pacing up and down in the next bedroom. Obviously the choice he had to make was playing on his mind. The next day, José asked him if he'd come to any conclusions.

'Can you really help me with my travelling expenses and get the necessary documents for me?' Cesar's face was eager.

'Of course.'

'And you would pay my fees through seminary?'

'Yes; that's what I told you.'

'O.K., I'll go.'

It was a decision that was to change the whole course of Cesar's life.

* * *

The ring of the telephone in my office interrupted my work.

'Peter, I have just heard that Editorial Caribe is being merged with another Christian publishing company there in Mexico.'

It was Jonas Ramirez, head of a special programme to evangelize the whole of Latin America. He was calling from the mission headquarters in Costa Rica.

'That's right,' I confirmed. The decision had only recently been made, and I wasn't yet sure where I would fit into the new plan.

'Perhaps this is the time for you to move on to a new challenge,' Jonas continued. 'We need an adviser for our evangelism programme in Colombia. It will be tough, because of the problems there, but I feel you are the man for the job.'

I felt my heart skip. I had to admit that I had missed being out there on the front line as an evangelist. By now the publishing work had grown dramatically and I had an efficient team of helpers working with me.

'Let me call you back, Jonas. I must pray about this.'

That night I shared the phone conversation with my Chiquita.

'Does that mean we would have to leave Mexico?' she asked.

'It would.'

She considered for a moment.

'O.K., Peter; wherever you go, I will be at your side.'

As we had our Bible reading together, I came across Isaiah 54:2. It read: 'Enlarge the place of your tent, and let the curtains of your habitations be stretched out; hold not back, lengthen your cords and strengthen your stakes.'

I turned to Blanca. 'It seems as if the Lord wants us to enlarge our vision,' I chuckled. 'The world is bigger than just Mexico, and Jesus did command us to go into all the world. I'm sure we should go to Columbia. After all, we won't be the first.' Blanca looked puzzled. 'Well, the country is named after Christopher Columbus. He beat us there by a few hundred years.' I laughed aloud and gave my wife a hug.

As a final confirmation that I should be back in evangelism, I was asked to be president of a crusade committee for David Wilkerson, author of the best-selling book *The Cross and the Switchblade*, and founder of the Teen Challenge ministries for drug addicts. The crusades were in Mexico City and Puebla, and many came to Christ during the meetings. I boarded the plane for Bogota with a joyful heart. I was ready again to break through new barriers.

* * *

I stood peering out from my second-floor bedroom window at the amazing scene below. I could see clearly a group of young *gamines* (street children who live by thieving) receiving special training for their villainy.

We had moved to the city of Cali, in the western part of Colombia, and in front of our house was a large open piece of ground.

One of the *gamines* (pronounced 'ga-mean-eys', from the French word meaning 'urchin'), who looked only about four, was learning how to snatch a pen from the pocket of an unsuspecting tourist. He had a ball of loose hemp fibres hidden behind his back and the plan was to approach his victim slowly, jerk the ball of hemp up and across the pocket where the pen was clipped so the fibres would catch on the pen and then to kick his victim at the back of the legs so he would fall down. By the time the poor tourist had struggled to his feet the child would be gone.

Blanca came and stood by me.

'Fagin would have a ready-made army of young thieves here,' I murmured, thinking of Charles Dickens's *Oliver Twist*. 'Can you believe that this sort of thing is still going on in 1968?' We were transfixed by the scene.

'You know, Chiquita, there are thousands of these *gamines* all over the country. They have no place to live and only survive by their wits. They steal, lie, and cheat. They'll strip the watch off your arm, the glasses from your face, and the belt from your pants before you can shout "*policia*".'

I told Blanca that I had heard that each of these children belonged to a specific gang.

'El Perro (the dog), as the *gamines*' leader is called, assigns the jobs. It may be stealing, begging, shining shoes, selling newspapers, or stripping windscreen wipers off cars. At the end of the day each *gamine* must bring his earnings to the gang and turn them over to El Perro, who then distributes equal shares among all the workers.'

I was soon travelling all over this beautiful country, with its towering mountains and lush green valleys.

As I drove towards another city for a crusade meeting, I would pass colourfully dressed Indians on their way to market, their wares packed tightly on the backs of loping mules.

One night I preached to a packed congregation in a remote town on the west coast. We had reached the community in a dug-out canoe, which we had had to rent, along with the men to paddle it.

At the end of the service, I issued the altar call. Many came to the front of the church to make their commitment to Christ.

I saw one young man hesitate when I invited the congregation to make their commitment to Christ. Later he came over to me. 'Sir, I want to become a Christian, but I am single. That is my problem.'

I was surprised.

'But why is being single a problem?'

'Sir, it is a terrible problem. For that reason I cannot accept Christ.'

He shook his head sadly and shuffled out of the building.

The pastor of the church had overheard the conversation, and seeing my puzzlement, took me on one side.

'Brother,' he explained, 'that young man said he was single. What he really meant was that he wasn't married. He was ashamed to tell you that he has three women living with him. None of them, however, is his official wife. He knows that if he becomes a Christian, he will have to make a choice about which one to marry. Two would have to go. He's not prepared to make that decision yet.'

Next morning, I was carrying my small bag down the road to the river so I could be paddled to the next village. The silence was broken abruptly by the squeal of brakes and a sickening thud. A Jeep had struck a young man, who toppled backwards like an axed tree. A woman, presumably his wife, began to scream in a high and strangled voice. The baby strapped to her back soon joined in.

I watched, hardly daring to breathe, as an oversized man clambered out of the Jeep and ambled over to the injured youth.

'You stupid animal,' he yelled. 'Why don't you watch where you are going? Didn't you see me coming?'

A dozen chickens clucked and ran in all directions, fluttering their useless wings, while the injured figure just lay there face down, moaning.

'You people are so stupid.'

With that, the driver stormed back into his vehicle and drove off at high speed, leaving a trail of dust behind him.

I tried to comfort the distraught young wife, swallowing my fury at the behaviour of the driver.

Later, I told the pastor about the incident.

'Peter, this sort of thing happens here all the time,' he told me sadly. 'I know who that driver was – the owner of a large fruit plantation on the edge of town, an American. He doesn't look upon our people as human at all. They are just there to help pick the fruit and make him even richer.'

I couldn't believe it.

'Are there others like that around here?'

'Not just here, but all over my country. They come in from many developed countries and exploit the people. They rape our country.'

I was horrified, and began to wonder what the Church was doing to help. Was it there only to pander to the rich and preserve the status quo? Did the Gospel have answers for such exploitation? Should we work to change society or just preach the Gospel? These were questions that nagged me.

When I finally returned to my office, it was with a heavy heart. The more I saw in Colombia, the more confused and angry I became.

*   *   *

One of the highlights of each day in the Cali office was the mail delivery. I always enjoyed receiving a letter from my family back in Mexico. So when one afternoon my secretary handed me an envelope in my mother's handwriting, I was overjoyed.

I tore it open anxiously and began reading.

'Dear son,' the letter began, 'I didn't want to send you this letter, but I feel I must. Twenty days ago your Grandfather Emilio was taken to the hospital with pneumonia and died shortly afterwards . . .'

I couldn't read any more. I just held my head in my hands and began to sob. After a while, I stumbled home, unable to face staying in the office.

I told Blanca the news, and we wept together.

When I calmed down a little, I shared something else with her.

'Just before I left, Grandpapa Emilio told me not to go to Colombia. He said that I would never see him alive again if I did. I told him not to be silly; not to talk in that way. But still he insisted. Now, what he said has come true. Maybe we shouldn't have come here after all.'

*   *   *

Death and violence were constantly on my mind in Colombia, and questions about a Christian's response to exploitation continued to disturb me.

I was in Bucaramanga taking a week of meetings. Luis, one of the converts of the crusade, took me one afternoon into an ice-cream parlour before the evening service.

A young man joined us, and Luis introduced me.

'This is the evangelist I was telling you about, Javier. He was the one who led me to Christ.'

I could see the young man wince.

'My friend Peter,' Luis continued fervently, 'has assured me that Jesus is the answer to every problem.'

'To every problem?' Javier's question was barbed. 'To the problem of exploitation, poverty, and the abuses of the rich towards the poor? Does Jesus have the answer to that?'

I nodded. 'Yes, because He changes the hearts of men from which come all the ambition and the hatred that bring about these terrible things.'

'I don't believe it.' Javier's voice shook with bitterness. 'Religion has been supporting the wealthy class here in Colombia. The machine gun is the only answer. It is the only way to bring justice.' With that he brandished his clenched fist in the air and stormed out through the door.

'He is a member of an urban guerrilla group,' Luis told me.

That night, after the evening service, an old lady hobbled over to me.

'Young man, I have come here tonight because I have been told that I can be healed of a tumour in my right leg. Is that true?'

I was a little taken aback with the question. I had never prayed for healing for anyone before.

'Well, the Bible does say that God has all power and I am sure He can heal you.'

Her face lit up.

'Just wait there a moment,' I said, 'and I will get the pastor to come and pray for you.'

I interrupted the pastor who was deep in conversation with a group of young people. He peered over his glasses at me.

'Why ask me, Peter? Don't you believe that God can heal her?'

'Yes, but I've never prayed for –'

'If you believe, you should pray for her.'

With much fear and trepidation, I laid hands on the frail woman and prayed for her healing. At that moment I realised once more that it was no good for me just to know the Bible in theory, I had to put what it said into practice. I had to claim its many promises.

That night I lay on my bed and read for the umpteenth time verses 18 and 19 of Luke 4:

'The spirit of the Lord is upon me, because He has annointed me to preach good news to the poor. He has sent me to proclaim release to the captives and recovering of sight to the blind, to set at liberty those who are oppressed, to proclaim the acceptable year of the Lord.'

I lay back on my pillow and thought of how I had become

a great talker, but had done little or nothing to help 'release the captives' of poverty and oppression.

I, like many other Christians, had shied away from any involvement in subversive movements that aimed at changing society, even if that required violent action.

Why?

I didn't know the answer at that time.

With that burden on my heart, I returned to Cali and shared with Blanca all the disturbing things I had seen and heard.

'Hundreds came to the Lord, Chiquita, yet I have come to feel that something is missing in my ministry.'

She moved up close to me.

'Perhaps God is trying to teach you something. Let's ask Him what it is.'

We sank to our knees.

'Lord, you know my heart at this time. What is next? What do you want me to do to serve the impoverished people of this tragic continent? Just show me what I should do.'

14. Which Revolution?

The constant vibration of the jet engines almost lulled me to sleep. After one traumatic year in Colombia, I was returning to Mexico, to be involved in similar work in my home country.

Olympic fever had hit the world and I had been following the events in the press with great interest. The paper I was reading carried the usual list of results in the 'cold war' between the American and Russian athletes.

Part of the way down page one I began reading the latest charges and counter-charges made by students and government officials about an alleged massacre that had taken place three weeks earlier in Mexico City, in which an estimated 600 died. The violence had erupted when students in the capital had tried to halt the games. They were pressuring the government for better conditions at universities, more opportunities for poor people to attend, and better teaching staff. Students across the land had gone on strike. The mass killings were the culmination of weeks of trouble.

I leaned over to Blanca and showed her the news item.

'I hope Ruben wasn't involved in that. He was a student delegate from Monterrey to try to negotiate with the government.' I wondered if my brother realised how dangerous was his part in the student campaign against the government.

'What if he was one of the victims?' My worry turned to fear.

'Ladies and gentlemen, please fasten your seat belts. We

are about to land at Mexico City International Airport.'

I shut my eyes and waited for the moment when the wheels struck the ground and the plane screeched along the runway as it braked.

I was relieved to find Nellie, my eldest sister, waiting behind the barrier. She would know if Ruben was all right.

We rushed into each other's arms as the air terminal's echoing loudspeakers relayed flight messages.

'Sister, I've been reading about the troubles here. How is Ruben?'

She read the troubled look on my face.

'He's fine,' she reassured me. 'He did come here for part of the protest, but fortunately he had returned to Monterrey when the massacre took place.'

'Thank God, he's safe,' I whispered. 'Thank God.'

We planned to spend the day with Nellie and her husband Samuel, an evangelical minister. They now had a lovely daughter. As we drove over there, Nellie told us of the new venture she'd embarked upon.

'I am now the scriptwriter for a Christian radio programme called 'From Heart to Heart'. Each week we dramatise a problem from daily life and then we show how Christ can answer it.'

Before I realised it, I was shouting at Nellie. 'Do you think Christ was the answer for those dead students? Will you be doing a programme about them?'

She didn't answer. I could see she didn't want a confrontation with me. We had never argued before.

'What is making you angry, Peter?' Nellie said at last in a soft, placatory tone.

I tried to explain what I'd seen in Colombia.

'I don't feel I can just play games any more, sister. There is a life and death struggle for justice going on in Latin America.'

Blanca desperately tried to steer the conversation around to more mundane matters. But I wouldn't be deterred.

'Do you know, Nellie, we even got robbed in Colombia a week before we left to come home!' I explained that we had

113

put an advertisement in the local paper saying we were leaving and wished to sell our furniture.

'A sweet old lady arrived. She liked the furniture and asked if she could pay us in U.S. dollars. I was delighted. She brought out of her purse $1,500 in large notes and handed them to me. We were almost broke and this was a windfall for us.

'Shortly afterwards, a van arrived to take away the furniture she had bought. That night I was checking over the money when I noticed that the serial numbers were all the same. I jumped into my car and drove to the address she had given me. It didn't exist! Then I checked with the American Embassy and they confirmed that I had been given forged dollars. It was a terrible blow!'

'But,' interrupted Blanca, 'do you remember what I told you? When we move somewhere we always seem to start with nothing. So we're just keeping up the tradition.'

Suddenly my rage was spent. My lovely wife had brought me down to earth again with a loving bump. I felt a twinge of remorse for my aggressiveness.

The next day we returned to Monterrey, where I was to be based for the next twelve months, helping to organise evangelistic outreach into my massive country. It was a time that I later felt was most worthwhile, and culminated in my being invited to be a delegate to the Latin American Congress of Evangelism in Bogota, Colombia, sponsored by the Billy Graham Evangelistic Association.

It was there I received the invitation to call in at the United Bible Society offices in Mexico City before returning to Monterrey.

Ken Bystrom, the head of the Training and Distribution Department, apparently needed a new assistant.

*   *   *

We talked excitedly when I entered Ken's office. We'd known each other for years. Ken had previously been a missionary in Venezuela, and I had come to respect him and his wife greatly.

'The job I want you to do,' he explained, 'is to organise seminars so that people can evangelize with the Bible.'

'The sort of thing I was doing for the Bible Society?'

'Well, much more than that. There you were training lay people. Now we want you to teach pastors, other leaders and, of course, our representatives.'

'You mean in Mexico?'

'Of course not, Peter. I know you have a wide vision and this will be your chance to serve the Church from Mexico to the other end of this continent.'

I was puzzled.

'But why did you choose me, Ken?'

He then fished out from his desk drawer a copy of an illustrated Bible Society booklet I had written years before, entitled *The Follow-up Training Booklet*. In it, I outlined how the Bible could be used in evangelism.

'I contacted you because of this: I came across it recently and I think these ideas are just what we want. You seem to know exactly what needs to be done.'

I couldn't deny that I was delighted to receive such an invitation. It seemed God was again calling Blanca and me to 'expand our tents'. With my wife's wholehearted consent, I agreed to take up the post at the beginning of January.

'That will be a good start to 1970 for both of us,' was Ken's enthusiastic response to the decision.

* * *

'Peter, come and sit down. I have a serious problem to discuss with you.' Ken had spread out before him a newspaper outlining the troubles in Chile. Dr. Salvador Allende, the leader of the extreme left Socialist Party, had joined in a Popular Union with the more moderate pro-Soviet Communists and several other factions, and had secured the presidency with a small plurality and only 36.3 per cent of the popular vote.

'There are now widespread strikes and disorders in the country,' Ken told me. 'I know we were planning for you to

115

take a seminar in Chile, but now I wonder if it is safe for you to go.'

Up until then, I had travelled for more than three years with the United Bible Societies all over Latin America without serious incident. But the increased violence troubled me.

'Why don't we contact the head of the Bible Society there, and see what he says?' suggested Ken. 'If he feels that it is not only dangerous for you to be there, but also dangerous for the pastors to take part, we'll call it off.'

By telephone from Santiago I was told how bad the situation was.

'There are demonstrations in the streets and we believe a full-scale revolution could break out at any moment. We want you to come, but you must know the risk. As far as the pastors go, they want to have this training. They believe that this is the hour for aggressive evangelism in our strife-torn country.'

'All right, brother, I'll come.'

I felt my stomach tighten at what I had agreed to do, and asked Ken to get the 'Prayer Warriors' out in force for me and the brethren in Chile. I knew that this trip could be extremely dangerous.

I had become firmly convinced that only Christ's saving power could bring about change in a land of such strife and injustice. At one stage, I'd been inclined to side with the idea of violent protest, but Christ's way forward had become clear to me one evening in conversation with Blanca.

'I am sure,' I mused, 'that when Jesus was on this earth, he lived in a society that was even worse than the one we find in Latin America right now. The Jews were a conquered and humiliated people. Yet He never once told His disciples to take up the sword and fight the oppressors. No, He was against that.'

Blanca picked up her Bible and read John 8:32. 'You will know the truth and the truth will make you free.' Then she turned to verse 36: 'So if the Son makes you free, you will be free indeed.'

That was it! The inner man, the heart, had to change before justice could be brought about. Only someone who was free in Christ could change his attitude and treat others with love and fairness.

When I arrived at Santiago airport the mood there was grim. I queued to go through customs, and began to think about a paperback book I had just read, called *God's Smuggler*. It told the astonishing story of a Dutchman named Brother Andrew who had for years been smuggling Bibles and other Christian literature into Eastern Europe.

I had been greatly challenged by his story, but hadn't seen any relevance in it for Latin America. I knew that things were rough for believers in that Communist-controlled part of the world, but the Church in my continent appeared to have great freedom.

Suddenly, the voice of the customs officer broke into my thoughts.

'Do you have anything to declare?' I was conscious I was under observation from hostile eyes.

'Well, just some Christian materials and Bibles.'

His look convinced me that he did not approve. After all, he was the representative of an extreme left-wing government. But this wasn't Eastern Europe. Surely, there wouldn't be any problems!

'We don't need that sort of stuff here,' he said scornfully. 'We have enough of that nonsense already. It's bad for the people.' His voice was curiously low and unpleasant.

I thought I was hearing things. The way he was reacting he could have been a guard on the Russian border.

'Lord,' I silently whispered in a telegram prayer, 'please give me the wisdom you gave that Dutchman when he crossed through hostile frontiers.'

The official became impatient. 'Are you deaf or something?'

'I'm sorry, sir. But it won't do any harm, will it? It's just for a few friends.' I tried to look nonchalant, but by now my heart was hammering in my chest.

Amazingly, he relented, and impatiently waved me through.

117

The tension in Chile at that time was almost unbearable. There was an electricity in the air you could almost touch. Soldiers with automatic weapons were everywhere around the airport.

My contact from the Bible Society came to pick me up in a mini-bus. We were stopped several times at road blocks on our way into town.

'Peter, thank you for coming. The leaders here are aware of the dangers, but they are awaiting the seminar with great expectation.'

After he had dropped me off at my hotel, I freshened up and went into the restaurant for a meal.

The waitress came over and I pointed to the menu.

'I understand you have good steaks here,' I said.

She lowered her eyes.

'We did, sir. But not now. All I can offer you from the whole menu is vegetable soup with cheese sandwiches. We have terrible shortages these days.'

She seemed afraid to say any more. So later I decided to go into the streets to see for myself what was happening. Just a short way from the hotel, right in the middle of Santiago, I came across a huge crowd of people chanting, 'We want food . . . we want food . . .'

I began elbowing my way through the mass of people and soon got caught up in the fervour of the situation.

'Down with Allende, down with Allende!' they cried.

'Say, why aren't you joining in?' one man asked me.

I mumbled something about being a visitor from Mexico, and decided to head for the edge of the crowd. There was an ugly feeling in the air, and I was getting worried. I knew that at any moment Allende's thugs could make a baton charge or even fire into the crowd.

The seminar was to run for one week. On the first morning some seventy-five pastors and Christian leaders turned up.

One of them told me how glad he was that I had come.

'Most of the evangelism I have been practising is the kind where we invite people to come into our services to hear the Gospel. But people today don't want to come. We need to go out to where they are, onto the streets, into the bars, and share with them the Good News of Jesus Christ at this terrible time in Chile's history.'

Each afternoon, I would join with one of the pastors in taking the message out to the streets. On the first day, the pastor I was accompanying got involved with a student who was seething at what was happening in the country.

'We were promised justice, but now we starve. There are hardly any jobs left because most of the big companies have closed down and left.' He looked at the large Bible I was clutching. 'What does your Bible teach about justice in this situation?'

I was reminded of the young urban guerrilla I had met in Colombia. 'Are you asking me if violence is the answer?' I began. 'I believe it is not. I believe the only justice that you can get is from God. He can give you a change of heart and then you will have a new attitude and not want to kill and maim others to get your own way. The big problem I see in Chile, as in many countries, is that you have put your trust in a man. No man can bring real justice. If Allende fails, who knows if the man that replaces him will be any better? None of us knows.'

I turned and pointed to the pastor. 'This man is one of many who believe there is an alternative to what is going on here at this time. It is a revolutionary alternative based on love.'

By now the young man was listening intently.

'But that still doesn't put food in my belly,' he argued.

I had to agree.

'Not in the short term. But which is more important to you – to be well fed in this life or have life forever? If you give your heart to Jesus Christ, not only will you benefit but so also will those around you. You will no longer feel anger and hatred towards others. Your attitude towards them will be different. You will start a new dynasty. Why not try it?'

I expected a tirade, but just the opposite occurred.

'Well what are you waiting for? Help me to do it!'

We took him into a little alleyway and he made his decision for Christ. We both hugged him, and I said,

119

'Welcome to the Kingdom, brother. You are now part of the royal family.'

The young man began attending this pastor's church and for a time I forgot all about him. But then on September 11th, 1973, came the news that the military forces had decided to overthrow the government. In the brutal battle that followed, Salvador Allende was either killed or committed suicide.

When I heard the news, I offered up a prayer for my new friend.

'Lord, please help him to be at the forefront of the healing process that now has to take place in Chile. Help him to "preach good news to the poor, proclaim release to the captives, set at liberty those who are oppressed, and proclaim the acceptable year of the Lord." That is my great wish. That, Lord, is the *real* revolution.'

15. Prophets of Revolution

The secretaries crowded around my desk as I took off my jacket and settled down to do battle with the mountain of mail that awaited me.

'How did the trip go, Peter? Tell us all about it.'

It had become a tradition that I would give an informal account of my latest journey to the girls who worked in the offices of the United Bible Societies. They would not let me settle until I had told all. So, as usual, I heaved an exaggerated sigh and then got on with it.

I had just begun my latest report when I noticed a new girl watching me intently. I stopped momentarily and let out a gasp. 'Olivia, what are you doing here? I thought you were in Germany!'

It was my young sister whom I had not seen for two years. Her skin was radiant, her eyes were bright. She was still petite and slender, but was now growing into a beautiful woman.

'I am working in the translations department of the Bible Society on the popular version of the Old Testament,' she replied, her eyes alight with enthusiasm.

I smiled broadly. 'My sister, welcome to the happy family of the Bible Society.'

Later, I walked round to her office, and found her consulting a Greek version of one of the books of the Bible. Spread across her desk was a litter of old tomes and manuscripts.

'How can you understand any of those different languages?'

Olivia grinned. 'Peter, I have already learned English, German, French, Greek and Hebrew.'

I was stunned.

We laughed together when she added: 'But I still keep on thinking that Spanish is the heavenly language!'

I settled down to catch up on the news. Olivia told me that as soon as her project was finished, she would be returning to the University of Costa Rica to take a degree in languages. Hearing of Costa Rica brought Cesar to mind, and I questioned Olivia urgently. 'Hasn't Cesar just been appointed international coordinator for the youth movement, Minamundo (Ministry to the Student World)?'

She nodded. 'Yes, he should be very good with the students. But I think he must have changed a bit. Did you know that when he was a student at the seminary he nearly provoked a student strike? I was there at the time.'

I shook my head in disbelief. 'I never heard that. What happened?'

'Cesar was president of the student body during his last year. He had become much more politically aware of the situation in Latin America, and had taken a theological option that related to the more oppressed and isolated sectors of our society. Then he found the curriculum of the seminary was quite out of date and not as relevant to Latins as it claimed to be.'

The words poured out as if a cork had been pulled from her. I could see that she, too, was heavily committed to these ideas.

'Most of the teachers were North American and were still teaching us with concepts from their culture. They also taught us Bible study methods in the traditional North American way, instead of taking into consideration our different upbringing. There were also several courses that were out of place and were taught to us by teachers who didn't know our culture in depth at all.'

There was now high colour in Olivia's cheeks as she told me that Cesar also opposed the way that study was organised for the final comprehensive exam.

'The students would go into the room to take their exams

122

so tired after many hours of study and revision that they would have black marks under their eyes. Cesar felt this should also end. It seemed the more he looked into the running of the seminary the more angry he became. There was no student representation on the faculty, and the teachers seemed to assume automatically that they were always right in their thinking.

'The situation got so bad that Cesar threatened them with a student strike. He told the faculty, "We are all going to leave if this doesn't change." Many of us, to show we meant business, began to pack our suitcases.

'Finally they gave in and substantial changes were made. It was quite a victory for Cesar. But many of the teachers didn't take it well and wouldn't speak to our rebellious brother for a long time after that.'

Her eyes shone with pride as she added: 'Now many of them admire him. They feel he was a person of great courage. And he was!'

I hardly recognised this Cesar as the soft-spoken brother I had known, and I sought him out, intrigued, when I was next in Costa Rica.

We met in his office: he didn't look any different. He was as affectionate as ever, but there was a glint of determination in his eye and an urgency in his voice.

'How did your time with Minamundo in Colombia go?' I asked, knowing what a profound effect my time in that country had had on me.

'Peter,' he said, 'I saw the worst poverty I have ever seen in my life. I was working in the Atlantic Coast area. The people lived in hovels, with pigs and dogs sharing their home, while the rich lived in big houses with plenty to eat and many servants.'

A flush of anger darkened his face as he continued: 'Many in the Church would have nothing to do with the poor. They didn't want to work with them at all. That made me mad.' He ran his hands through his hair. 'I had to try and change it. I wanted these people to be real men and women made in the image of God. Not, as they were then, half or incomplete. I wanted them to have hope.'

123

So Cesar began to work on their behalf by trying to find jobs for the unemployed, teaching them simple health care and sanitation.

'I did all this while preaching the Gospel to them,' he explained. 'I felt both had to go hand in hand. I know I was supposed to be there to work with the students, but when I saw the situation I just had to get involved.'

I soon discovered that Cesar wasn't the only activist in the family. Back in Mexico City, I went over for a meal with Ruben and his wife, Magdalena. They had moved into a modest apartment in the capital so that he could study for his master's degree in law and later for his doctorate. To help them survive financially, he had also taken a job with a government department, set up to help peasants who specialised in rural arts and crafts.

As Ruben travelled the country to organise these badly exploited workers into co-operatives and unions, he found himself incensed with the way they had been trapped for generations by the greed of others.

'I discovered that the chief of the area, often the mayor, would lend money to craftsmen so they could buy their raw materials,' Ruben told me. 'He would charge high interest rates and soon the men were trapped. A man can be indebted all his life; then he is easy to exploit. I decided that I had to try to break this bondage and organise them. We created stores for the craftsmen to sell their goods directly to the public instead of through people who were going to cream off most of the profit.

'It is dangerous work, because often the local chief will try to stop me operating by using all sorts of threats. And sometimes the workers can't understand what I am doing and criticise me. Eventually, though, the schemes begin to work, and the artisans start to benefit. I feel the whole plan is worthwhile. I am, at last, able to help my people.'

It was extraordinary how my family was becoming a force for change. In our different ways we were all 'prophets of revolution'. Like the prophets in the Bible, we were impelled almost against our will. Whether we liked it or not, we were involved in the very fabric of life in Latin

America.

But we weren't the first generation in our family to be revolutionary. My grandfather on my mother's side was once the richest man in town, but gave up everything to join Pancho Villa's revolution against the dictator, General Victoriano Huerta. He was trusted enough by Villa to be appointed one of his treasurers, and he saw the ultimate overthrow of Huerta.

Then there was my great-grandfather who was one of the first converts of the American Evangelical missionaries. He took the Good News on horseback to all the surrounding areas, being careful to take food with him as well as his Bible. Often, he wouldn't give the food openly to the people he preached to but would slip back later, under cover of darkness, and leave it on their doorstep. He didn't want people to accept the Gospel in gratitude to him. He wanted them to be convinced that it was true and important for them. There was terrible persecution of Protestants at that time, but my great-grandfather wasn't deterred from his spiritual revolution. He continued until his death at the age of ninety.

So we had a rich heritage. Each one of us had grabbed the flag. And each of us was acting according to the leading of God.

16. The Battle for Lima

Eerie silhouettes of soldiers moved urgently about the edge of the terminal at the Lima International Airport.

'Can you see the outline of their weapons?' asked Hermano Pablo, (Paul Finkenbinder) the well-known Latin evangelist, with whom I was now working as executive director of his radio, television and crusade ministry.

'It looks as if there's trouble here,' I murmured in reply.

A spirit of revolution was sweeping through Latin America like a brush fire. Bloody confrontations were inevitable because military dictatorships were brutally trying to stem the tide of change. Each side vied with the other in cruelty to their victims.

I noticed that only five people disembarked from the Boeing 707 that had brought us to the Peruvian capital. I was travelling with the evangelist and Manuel Bonilla, the famous Mexican Gospel singer. We were in Lima for a crusade which had been planned for several months.

At the immigration desk I presented my passport. Standing at the official's side was a soldier, his finger on the trigger of his gun.

'What's going on?' I asked the grim-faced immigration official. He didn't reply, but stamped my passport and handed it back to me.

'Just go through,' he said roughly.

Then followed the customs search, again under the beady eye of a soldier, his rifle at the ready. This was the most thorough inspection I had ever encountered in Latin America.

When the official had finished poking about in my luggage he turned to me and said, 'I'm afraid, sir, there are no taxis running at this time. You will have to call your hotel in Lima and they will have to arrange transport for you. Just make the call and then wait outside.'

As we waited for our bus to arrive from the town, we wondered if the crusade, scheduled to begin later that very day in the main bull ring, could still go ahead. As we talked, a jackbooted soldier strutted by.

'Excuse me, sir,' I asked him, 'but can you tell me why no taxis are running?'

'Don't you know we have a curfew from ten p.m. until five o'clock in the morning?'

I didn't. And it was now one a.m.

'Doesn't that mean it will be dangerous for us to travel into Lima at this time?'

He shrugged his shoulders.

'Right now it is dangerous anywhere in Peru.'

Soon the hotel bus arrived and we clambered aboard. After about three miles, bumping along the darkened highway into the city, the driver suddenly slammed his foot on the brake.

I had been dozing on and off, but was now jolted back into reality. A huge gun from a tank was pointing directly at the windscreen. Two Jeeps pulled up outside the two doors of the bus, and soldiers poured out, aiming their weapons at our heads.

Then one jerked open the door and barked, 'What are you people doing on this road? Don't you know there is a curfew?' I froze, not daring to move.

'Passports! Let's see them!'

The three of us quickly produced our travel documents and handed them to him.

'Where is your permit to be out at this time of night?'

'We are just coming from the airport,' I managed to stammer out. 'I don't think they gave us one there.'

Impatiently he flipped through my passport, and a piece of yellow paper dropped out and fluttered to the ground.

'That's it; you are O.K. It's your permit. You may proceed.'

The perspiring driver waited for the army tank to move back and then slowly eased the vehicle around it.

We finally went to sleep that night to the sound of gunfire from all over the city. Next morning all seemed quiet when we gathered for breakfast with Julio, the local co-ordinator for the crusade. He looked very distressed.

'I am so sorry, my friends, but the crusade is off. Last night, a revolution took place and a new junta seized power. They have already issued a decree that no public meetings can take place. They are expecting trouble and don't want people to gather in any numbers.'

It was a blow for all of us. The planning for this Hermano Pablo crusade had gone on for six months. Many pastors had co-operated in it. It had seemed a great force for unity in the capital. But now all the good work was lost. We needed to pray about the situation. So there, at that hotel breakfast table, amid much clatter of eating and talking, we asked God to show us what we should do in this confused situation.

'I know we are here for a purpose, Lord, and I know that we are here so that the Gospel may be preached,' I said. 'Please just show us what we have to do. We are completely in your hands.'

After we had all prayed, our Peruvian friend said he would see if anything could be done. 'I'll be in touch with you as soon as I have some news.'

When he returned, we all gathered in Pablo's room. It had been a short vigil of waiting.

'I have good news for you,' Julio said, a grin spreading over his tanned face.

'I have made contact with a Christian in the military and he says we can have a meeting here in this very hotel, for businessmen and leaders of the community. He has promised to come personally to guarantee there will be no problems with the new government.'

'But won't that take a long time to arrange?' I asked.

He smiled.

'Brothers, all the plans have already been made; the invitations have gone out. We have been working hard and now we expect the Lord really to bless our efforts.'

Hermano Pablo was very pleased.

'Thank you, Julio, for your help in this. I suppose after this meeting we will have to leave.'

'Brother,' he said, a pained look on his face, 'please don't talk like that. We have also arranged for you to preach all week at the biggest churches in Lima. The people will come in large numbers because of the troubles. They will want to know if there is an answer to all the problems.'

The three of us came down half an hour before the meeting was due to start, just to check if anyone had actually come.

'Look at all those people,' whistled Hermano Pablo, as he saw the crowd going into the hotel room.

We were incredulous.

'I hope we can get in,' I laughed.

An excited babble of conversation swept through the rooms as we walked in. The chatter quickly subsided and I began by introducing this much beloved preacher, whose voice was known all over Latin America because of his radio ministry.

Manuel Bonilla sang a selection of Gospel songs in his beautiful tenor voice and the audience in that stifling room were captivated. I noticed many soldiers were dotted around the room. Apparently they had come at the invitation of the Christian military man. They were most respectful and had taken off their hats and left their rifles in a safe place outside the room.

When Hermano Pablo began to preach, you could have heard a pin drop. He opened his Bible at Luke 12:16 and announced that he would read through to verse 20.

Everyone listened respectfully. ' . . . the land of a rich man brought forth plentifully; and he thought to himself, "What shall I do, for I have nowhere to store my crops?" And he said, "I will do this: I will pull down my barns, and build larger ones; and there I will store all my grain and my goods. And I will say to my soul, 'Soul, you have ample goods laid up for many years; take your ease, eat, drink, be merry.' " But God said to him, "Fool! This night your soul is required of you; and the things you have prepared, whose will they be?" So is he who lays up treasure for himself, and is not rich toward God.'

He closed his large Bible. 'This passage doesn't just apply to those who have money,' he said, 'but also to those who are putting all their hopes in men or even religions made by men. All of you here, I am sure, are wondering what is going to happen in Peru. You are concerned to know if there is an answer to all these problems. Well, this morning, I want to tell you about a man who has the power to change all these negative things for good.

'I am talking about the One who could say to the storm, "Stop, be quiet," and it obeyed. A man who could tell the blind, "Now see," and they would recover their sight. A man who could tell the dead Lazarus, "Come forth," and he came alive.

'Who is this incredible man? His name is Jesus.'

At the end of the meeting, Hermano Pablo invited those packed into the room to hand over their lives to the Saviour. About a third of those present responded, many with tears in their eyes.

I felt like weeping myself as I saw soldiers standing stiffly to attention praying the 'sinner's prayer' and handing over their lives to their new Eternal Leader.

The week that followed was amazing. It was packed with services; hundreds accepted Christ. We left Lima for the airport with tears of gratitude to God in our eyes.

As the bus took us back to the terminal, I turned to my two friends and said, 'That certainly was a battle. We were right on the front line. Satan was really struggling to win this fight, but I know that he lost this time.'

I slipped my arm around Hermano Pablo's shoulders as a hot triumphant joy flashed through me.

'God won the battle for Lima this time, eh, brother?' I bubbled.

17. Brother Andrew's 'Wake-Up' Call

We were sitting down at home for an evening meal when Blanca turned to me.

'Hey, Peter, do you remember that book we read, called *God's Smuggler*?'

'Certainly, it was a good book.'

'Well, the author, Brother Andrew, is speaking at church tomorrow night.'

I was intrigued. I tried to picture what this Dutchman would look like. Would he be tall and dignified, or slight and determined?

'Let's go,' I told Blanca, 'and listen to this man who so much likes to swim against the current.'

Next night, our church was packed to capacity. I was surprised when a slim figure wearing a blue lightweight suit stood up, and with twinkling eyes began speaking. He had a lined face, yet I could imagine that many border guards would not have looked twice at him. He could lose himself in an instant in a crowd. Despite all he had been through, there was a likeable innocence in his features.

Brother Andrew asked us to turn to Revelations 3:2. 'Awake, and strengthen what remains and is on the point of death . . .'

The Dutchman then leaned forward and said in a surprisingly powerful voice, 'I want you all to WAKE UP!' I jumped in my pew as his words boomed out.

'I want you to wake up to the situation of your suffering

brothers and sisters around the world.'

He began to relate stories of persecuted believers he had visited all over Eastern Europe. Then he recounted how many had been imprisoned there for daring to follow Jesus Christ. He followed with a description of how the Marxist revolution had moved from Eastern Europe to China and South-East Asia, to Africa, and was now getting close to our sub-continent.

'Latin America is next on the map,' he said. 'You all here had better wake up before it is too late!'

Brother Andrew paused for a moment, then continued. 'I want you to know that there is a Church which is part of the same body that we belong to. It is a Church that is *our* responsibility. Their pain is *our* pain because we are members of the same body.'

He then read the second part of verse 3: 'If you will not awake, I will come like a thief and you will not know at what hour I will come upon you.'

That was like a knife to my heart.

'This is not an option, it's an order,' Brother Andrew said pointedly. He finished by reading verse 8: 'Behold, I have set before you an open door, which no one is able to shut.' He went on, 'None of you here has an excuse for not walking through that open door and serving your suffering brothers and sisters.'

With that he sat down. I remained in my seat, transfixed. I felt like a boxer who had just gone fifteen rounds with Mohammed Ali. His 'wake up' call was vibrating in my ears.

That night in bed, I shared my thoughts with Blanca.

'Chiquita, I wonder if I am really taking full advantage of that open door into Latin America? There may be much more I can do.'

*   *   *

'Daddy, there's a phone call for you,' called Nellie, my daughter, now fifteen years old.

It was Hermano Pablo.

132

'Peter.' His voice was choking with emotion. 'Have you heard the news about Guatemala?'

'I have, Pablo. I have just seen the terrible pictures on television. It looks as though thousands have died there.'

'Do you think there is anything we can do?' he asked urgently.

'My brother, Pablo, I feel we must do everything possible to help.'

He heaved a sigh of relief.

'Peter, that's wonderful. It is confirmation that I should get there as soon as possible and assess the need.'

As I put down the phone, more terrible pictures from the earthquake were flashed on the television screen. There I saw soldiers desperately trying to recover bodies from the tangled, twisted buildings, many of which had collapsed like a pack of cards.

'First reports,' said the newscaster, 'are that thousands have perished in the earthquake. It is the worst that has hit Guatemala for many years.'

I turned to Blanca and said, 'I have to admire Hermano Pablo. He isn't content just to preach to the people. I think he will have a great shock when he arrives in Guatemala City, but I know God will show him what he has to do.'

Next day, Hermano Pablo was on a plane into the earthquake zone, and three days later I met him at the airport. He was a totally changed person. He wept as he tried to tell us what he had seen and experienced.

'You can't imagine what it is like there. Thousands are buried under the rubble. The authorities are working day and night to try to rescue those that may still be alive, but it is a hopeless task. While I was there, a woman came up to me and said, "You have to help me. My baby is under there. He has been there for two days." What could I do, Peter? I asked her if I could pray for her so that she would find some relief from her torture. Then I had to tell her that there was no hope that she would see her baby alive. She had to accept that.'

I felt tears well up in my eyes. I had never seen my friend so affected by a situation before.

'We have to reorganise my ministry completely to help,' he said. 'I am going to make all my radio programmes to North America about Guatemala. I will do the same on television.'

Soon money and other relief aid came pouring in. The evangelist's television studio was transformed into a huge store room with clothing, blankets, medicine, food, and even tents by the score.

We chartered a DC6 cargo plane and loaded it full of relief items. We made two trips. Another fifteen tons of goods were sent by sea.

Two days after Hermano Pablo's first trip, I too headed off for the troubled land of Guatemala.

'Don't forget, Peter,' he had told me, 'we must make contact with the churches there and work through them. I want you not only to help co-ordinate the relief, but also to take time out to share the Good News with the people that survive.'

The spiritual hunger I found in Guatemala at that time was almost unbelievable. During the day I would be helping with the emergency relief, then at night I would speak at packed churches. People flocked to the front to accept Christ at my altar call. It seems that at a time of such desperate need, people do turn to God for answers.

I began to think back to Brother Andrew's challenge about walking through that 'open door'. Here I was, just a short time later, already involved in serving my brothers and sisters who were in anguish.

One night after a particularly distressing day, I had gone back to the hotel with my good friend, Woody Blackburn, the American photographer. He was in charge of Hermano Pablo's media department. As we sat in the coffee shop, the frightening tremors began again. The room was shaking so much that we had to pick our cups up off the table to prevent the coffee from spilling.

'I think perhaps we should get to bed early, Peter,' Woody said. 'You look exhausted.'

When we got to our room, we had a time of prayer for the people of Guatemala.

'Lord,' I prayed, 'we have been reminded, even tonight, of the great dangers that are still here in this country. Please, if it is your will, keep us safe while we are here.'

I laid my head on the pillow and within seconds I was in a deep sleep. At about three a.m. something woke me. The rumbling noise began again and I looked up at the wall behind my bed. Gradually, almost in slow motion, a long crack appeared, and as I watched a huge chunk of wall fell away towards my head.

Instinctively, I leaped off my bed and landed on Woody's. A split second later, the wall had completely crushed my bed.

'Errr . . . what's going on?' Woody spluttered, clawing his way back to consciousness. 'What are you doing on my bed? Go back to sleep, Peter.'

'But Woody, that wall just caved in and crashed on my bed. I was nearly killed.'

We switched on the light and surveyed the damage.

'All I can say, Woody, is that the angel of the Lord shook me just in time. He must really be "encamped around me".'

He shook his head. 'Peter, it's a miracle you're still alive.'

As we boarded the plane out of Guatemala City, I felt completely drained of emotion. Final figures showed that the devastating earthquake of 1976 left 26,000 dead, 76,000 seriously injured, and two million homeless.

Months later, a tornado ripped into the Mexican city of La Paz in the peninsula of Baja California. The tornado had caused a dam to break, and as the water hurtled through the poor part of town, shacks were just swept up and destroyed. People were caught in the flood and many hundreds drowned.

Nearby towns were also destroyed, and fishing boats had sunk like toys. Because fishing was the main industry of much of the area, this was a major disaster.

'Peter, we have to provide help,' Hermano Pablo told me once more.

After a reconnoitre of the stricken area with Woody

Blackburn, we decided to hire a DC3 to bring in emergency supplies. A committee was formed with the local pastors in La Paz so that we could channel all the relief through them.

One afternoon we were unloading supplies in Obregon, Sonora, a city not to far from the disaster area. We were concerned that those outside La Paz should also have help.

Manuel was quietly singing in Spanish, 'La Senda Milagrosa' (The Miraculous Pathway) and I had joined in, in harmony. We had often sung in this way in Hermano Pablo's crusades.

'Wow, what a sunset,' I marvelled as we watched the huge red ball sink below the horizon. 'This certainly has been another day that the Lord has made.'

Then suddenly, in my peripheral vision, I saw two vehicles appear out of the growing shadows. One was a car, the other a van. In an instant, eight men in civilian clothes jumped out of the vehicles and pointed rifles and automatic weapons at us. As we faced the gun barrels, their leader shouted in a high nasal voice, 'Stop, stop, immediately. Don't move!'

My heart stood still as the man screamed at Irving, the American co-pilot who was clambering back up the stairs into the plane, completely unaware of what was happening.

'*Alto! Alto! O Disparo.*' (Halt, halt, or I shoot.) The voice was cold and murderous. But Irving just kept going, not understanding what was being said.

At the top of my voice I yelled, 'Irving, stop! Stop! They're going to shoot you.' With that, he froze, and then slowly turned around.

Then the chief officer of this gun-toting group, who turned out to be members of the 'Judicial', a section of the secret police, barked, 'Who's in charge here?'

I lifted my hand.

'Where is your identification? I want everyone here to identify himself.'

Nervously, I dug out my passport and handed it to him. I also showed him the permits for the plane, and also a complete list of what we had, but he was obviously not convinced by our reason for being there.

'Right, you have to finish unloading the plane and then open every box that you have,' he instructed.

As we prised open the boxes and barrels, the police ripped the goods out of the containers and threw them to the ground. The more they found, the more angry they grew.

'Why are you bringing this stuff here?' the leader snapped.

I tried to appear calm. 'We have brought help to the little towns in this area. We found that everyone has been bringing relief just for La Paz . . .'

His attitude softened slightly.

'But we were tipped off that you were drug smugglers,' he said. 'We expected you to engage in a gun battle with us.'

He brought his unshaven face close to mine.

'Hey, my friend, you are very lucky that you didn't touch that camera around your neck.' I looked down at its telephoto lens.

'In the darkness, we thought it was a bazooka. See that man there?' I nodded. 'He had a machine gun pointed at your head the whole time. One false move and he would have blown your head off.'

I gulped.

'Well, you have to thank God that you didn't do anything foolish!'

After two hours we were finally cleared to make the delivery in the town.

Next morning we decided, before heading home, that we would fly low over other parts of the disaster area to see what was going on. It was a shocking situation. We saw flooding on a massive scale. Many houses were destroyed, and cattle dead. On the seashore we saw washed-up scraps of wrecked boats.

'The people have really suffered,' Manuel commented.

I added pointedly, 'You mean, *our* people have suffered.'

As we banked around the devastated area, we spotted an airstrip close by a town that looked particularly badly hit.

'Let's go down and see if we can help them in any way,' the pilot suggested.

'Fine by me.'

So he began his descent. But just as he got to the end of the runway, he cried out, 'Oh, no, there's gravel blocking the runway!'

I looked down and saw that at regular intervals, small piles of gravel, the same colour as the runway itself, were neatly stacked.

'It's too late to stop now. We're going down.' Just at the last minute, he managed to swerve from the runway, but then hit some sand and gravel at the side of it. We bumped along crazily for a short distance and then the wheels began sinking into the sand. The plane lurched to one side and stopped.

As we climbed out, I noticed hundreds of people running towards us. Word had got around that our plane was in trouble and I think the people expected us to crash.

Soon they surrounded us and began pumping our hands. We were taken to see the mayor of the town, who treated us royally.

'In the name of my people, I very much appreciate the risk you took to land to see what our needs were,' he told me.

Back at the airstrip, we had problems. First, we didn't know if we would be able to free the plane's wheels from the sinking sand. And then if we could, we weren't sure if there would be enough yards of gravel-free grass from which to take off.

'I have the answer,' said a young motor-cyclist. 'Let me go over the ground for you on my bike and then I will tell you the length you've got from my odometer.'

When the pilot heard the distance, he said, 'Well, if God gives us a miracle we can just about make it. But it will take just that.'

With that he started up the engine, and then gently backed up the plane. Amazingly, the wheels didn't jam in the sand. Soon we were as far back as we could go.

By now the crowds were at a safe distance, and he

shouted to us, 'Now you guys pray like you've never done before, and let's see if we can make it.'

He pushed the engines to full throttle, and we roared down the soft runway. It looked as if we were about to hit a fence at the edge of the field, when slowly, agonisingly slowly, we began climbing upwards.

I mopped the perspiration from my face with my sleeve and turned to Manuel.

'You know, Manuel, I have the feeling that there will not be too many more safe landings for us in Latin America . . .'

18. 'That They May Be One'

'Peter, I have to ask you a serious question.' Dr. Ralph Wilkerson, pastor of Melodyland, a large church in Anaheim, California, was speaking to me as I faced a committee of Christian leaders.

'What is it?'

'We would like to know what you consider to be the biggest problem of the Church in Latin America today.'

I looked at the group, which included David Du Plessis, Hermano Pablo, and Elmer Bueno, a charming television host. I knew they all had a deep concern for Latin America.

'Well,' I told them, 'I would say that the most serious problem is definitely the lack of unity. Everyone seems to be fighting each other. At this time, more than ever, Latin America needs a strong and united Church.'

Dr. Wilkerson nodded. 'We agree with you whole-heartedly. Can you help us with the co-ordination of the new 'John 17:21' ministry in Latin America?'

I was very happy with the request, knowing that this strange name actually had a profound meaning. It comes from the verse which reads, 'That they may all be one; even as thou, Father, are in me, and I in thee, that they also may be in us, so that the world may believe that thou hast sent me.'

The recently formed movement had been set up to try to heal the squabblings that so beset the Church. It was hoped it would encourage believers to forgive each other and then begin to love one another and work together effectively for the furtherance of God's Kingdom.

I told the committee that I would do my best to help, but I was already committed to Hermano Pablo's ministry.

'Brother Peter,' Pablo interrupted, 'I believe it is important to start this healing process; I willingly release you from some of your duties so you can begin the necessary travel.'

'John 17:21' had a disarmingly simple principle. It brought together Christian leaders in a particular area for an informal gathering lasting several days. In discussion, apparent differences between the leaders were seen for what they were: not really significant, and certainly not worth fighting over.

On our final day together, we would suggest the pastors asked God to forgive them for their bitterness towards each other, and then, if they felt able, to apologise to brothers there. Soon, pastors who had not spoken for years would hug each other and ask for forgiveness. It was a wonderful time of healing of relationships.

We began the programme in Colombia, then went on to Guatemala and Costa Rica. Soon a Christian television network began promoting the work, and the support it got in both North and South America was phenomenal.

Because interest grew so rapidly, the committee decided that 'John 17:21' should not be confined just to Latin America. A world-wide congress was planned for Singapore, and the Church leaders from all over the world were invited to attend. God had laid this principle on the hearts of many leaders.

One of the main speakers was to be Dr. Paul Yonggi Cho, pastor of the largest evangelical church in the world located in Seoul, Korea. He was also president of an organisation called Church Growth International, formed to share the experiences of his church which had grown at such incredible speed.

He told us that at that time (1978), he had about 100,000 members in his church.

'It all began because of the need for survival,' he revealed. I detected the same look of steel in his eyes as I had seen in Brother Andrew's. 'North Korea threatens us with invasion. We don't want our people just to survive, but to grow and continue the great commission of winning others for Christ.'

The Korean leader then outlined a unique cell system that had helped his church grow.

'We start with one cell of eight people, and when numbers in that cell reach sixteen, we split it in two. Then, when those two cells reach sixteen, the same happens again. Thus, not only do the members learn to survive, but also the church grows in a fantastic way. Each new cell is expected to have one new convert every month. So our growth now should be 8,000 new converts a month, since we have that many cells. The North Koreans could never stop the march of our church now.'

Bells began ringing in my mind. Surely, this kind of plan would work in Latin America.

'Would you come and teach this church growth method in Latin America?' I asked. Dr. Cho beamed. 'Of course I would. I would be delighted.'

The Singapore meetings went very well, and soon I was back in my region to prepare for Dr. Cho's visit. I became more and more involved in arranging Church Growth International seminars and also 'John 17:21' conferences.

By January 1979 much had been achieved across Central America. All had gone well until Nicaragua . . . but that's where we came in.

*   *   *

At that stage, the mindless violence I saw, the bickering between Church leaders, the eternal politics that beset the Church in Latin America – it was all getting me down.

I would lie in a lonely hotel room holding my head in my hands after another day of trying to reconcile Christian leaders or of seeing another act of killing. Sleep wouldn't come, and when I did fall into fitful dozing my dreams would be ugly and frightening. Slowly, I was sinking into despair.

At home, Blanca tried to comfort me, but the only

consolation I could find was in thinking of Jesus and how He had suffered for this crazy world. He knew what I was going through.

One day I yearned to talk to someone, really talk. I wanted to pour out my heart and share my anguish over Latin America. But one evangelist friend after another told me sympathetically that they were busy just then . . . perhaps another time. I felt completely isolated, locked in a terrible numbness.

Psalm 13, verses 1 and 2, could have been written from my own heart. 'How long, O Lord? Wilt thou forget me for ever? How long wilt thou hide thy face from me? How long must I bear pain in my soul, and have sorrow in my heart all the day? How long shall my enemy be exalted over me?'

I had reached the point of thinking that I didn't deserve even to live, when an American friend came to visit. Paul Northrup had been a missionary in Mexico for many years, and we had travelled together a great deal. He saw at once that something was badly wrong.

'Hey, what's the matter with you, Peter?'

His sympathetic voice almost wrung tears from me. 'Oh, my friend, I'm not sure I can handle it any more. Something has to change. I don't know what to do.'

Paul responded to the plea in my voice and took me out to the invigorating air of Laguna Beach where he encouraged me to tell him everything. There, I released all my pent-up emotions and shared all the hurt and confusion of the past weeks. Paul listened patiently, and we prayed together. I talked on, but already my sense of worthlessness was draining away. God was comforting me, teaching me something.

Then I stood up in the middle of that crowded beach and said out loud: 'Lord, I am handing everything back to you. All my pain, all my heartbreak. Please take it. I'm willing to do anything for you. Please let Jesus just live in me and use me in whatever way you want.'

As I finished my prayer, once again drawing on God's strength, I experienced a final release of tension. Joy flooded over me: the agony was over.

'It's not the end of my ministry after all,' I told Blanca later. 'I know God has a new beginning waiting for me.'

*　　*　　*

One week later a letter plopped through our mail box. I picked up the envelope and noticed it had on it the words, 'From Open Doors with Brother Andrew.'

'Chiquita,' I shouted, 'here's a letter from an organisation that uses Brother Andrew's name. It seems we can't escape from that guy.'

'Well, why don't you open it?' She became impatient. 'Let's see what it's all about.'

I ripped open the envelope.

Dear Mr. Gonzalez,

We have been looking for a co-ordinator for our Spanish work in Latin America and I recently mentioned this to Mr. José Becktol. He highly recommended you as someone who has a deep love and concern for the people of Latin America.

Would you please call me to set up a time when we could talk more about this?

It was signed by Dr. Dale Kietzman, a man I later discovered had worked for twenty-seven years with Wycliffe Bible Translators, both as an anthropologist and as an administrator. He had spent long years in Peru and Brazil.

This dignified man stood up when I entered his office in Orange, California. He asked me to take a seat.

'Peter, I am so pleased to meet you. I have heard much about you.'

I nodded nervously.

'I am sure you have heard about Open Doors?'

I felt my face blush red.

'I'm afraid I haven't. I don't know the first thing about the mission.'

'But surely you've heard of Brother Andrew?'

`'Oh, yes, I know he's the famous "God's Smuggler". I've read his book and heard him speak. I remember when he came to our church. His message had a real challenge for me.'

Dr. Kietzman then explained, 'Peter, this is his mission. It's designed to carry out Brother Andrew's vision to strengthen the Church in those parts of the world where it's suffering the most. And we wonder if you would accept our invitation to become part of the Open Doors family.'

I told him I wished to pray about it and to receive God's confirmation that this was the way He was directing me. So he pressed into my hand a collection of books and leaflets on the world-wide Open Doors ministry which serves the suffering and threatened churches in Eastern Europe, Africa, Asia, and now Latin America.

'Please let me know soon, Peter.'

That night I began reading through the materials and I saw that what this mission was trying to do was just what was needed in my part of the world. Again I found I was not alone in the burden I was carrying for Latin America. I also began to understand that the anguish I had just been through was not in vain. God had allowed me to go through it so that I could understand suffering at first-hand. I needed that experience to equip me to work hand-in-hand with my persecuted brethren in Latin America as part of Brother Andrew's ministry there.

I telephoned Dr. Kietzman.

'If you will have me, I am ready to join with you and Brother Andrew and the whole Open Doors team in this great battle. I am willing to walk through this open door for my people in Latin America.'

19. James Bond and the Sugarcane Curtain

I rapped nervously on the door of the hotel room in Santa Ana, California. There was no answer, so I tried again.

'That's strange,' I muttered to myself. I'd been told that Brother Andrew wanted to see me. Finally, the door opened and the slim figure of the famous 'smuggler' stood there. I introduced myself, and he ushered me into the room. We went and sat on the balcony. We looked nervously at each other, then at the passing cars below and then at each other again.

I was beginning to wonder whether he would eventually tell me all about his Bible-smuggling exploits.

'It's very warm today, Peter,' he finally said. 'Very different from my country.'

'Yes, it is very warm, Brother Andrew. Is Holland cold?

'It can be . . .' We spent several minutes in embarrassing small talk.

Finally I said, 'I read your book. I thought it was very good.'

He smiled wistfully. 'Yes, that all took place a long time ago now. But I'm still travelling for the Lord.'

We both nodded and then lapsed into silence. Although I couldn't understand what was going on, I was somehow glad that this much-respected man did not in any way try to impress me with stories of his incredible life. He seemed a very humble man.

Eventually I stood up to take my leave. I had spoken a little about Latin America, but I had really expected him to outline what he wanted of me in my new job.

'It was good to meet you, Brother Andrew. I hope to see you again.'

He nodded. 'I don't have any doubts about it. I'm sure we're going to see each other along the road.'

Later I told Dr. Kietzman about this puzzling interview.

'Dale, it wasn't an interview at all.'

Then it hit me.

'You know, Dale, I think he was expecting me to act like an expert on Latin America, and I was expecting him to tell me all about his accomplishments. We each had wrong expectations.'

We both threw back our heads and laughed heartily.

'But I have to say that I really liked the guy,' I continued. 'He was just like you and me.'

Dale then gave me my first serious assignment.

'Have you ever been to Cuba, Peter?'

'No, that's the one country I've always wanted to visit,' I told him.

Dale looked serious. 'Peter, we need you to go there to make new contacts. We've given help in various ways in the past, but we want to find out the needs of the Christians there now.'

I knew this would be a tough assignment, because I had read many stories of what had happened in that Caribbean island since 1959 when the bearded revolutionary, Fidel Castro, siezed power from the dictator Batista. I realised also that a communist government so closely tied to Russia could not look sympathetically upon churches that appeared to have links with North America. And most of the Protestant churches in Cuba had been the result of American missionary endeavour.

Blanca agreed to go with me on the trip. We went to a nearby bookshop and began buying the best Bibles we could find for the contacts we hoped to make there.

'Maybe,' said Blanca, 'you should get them some Christian books as well.'

I agreed and when the clerk added up the bill I discovered, to my surprise, that I had bought 200 Bibles and books.

'How are we ever going to fit that many into our suitcases?' Blanca asked as we struggled to carry the load out to our car.

I got out the largest suitcase I owned and carefully inserted the literature in between our clothing. I was inspired by the many James Bond films I had seen, packing and repacking the case as I thought 007 might have done it.

I hopped into bed at midnight a warm glow of self-congratulation flooding my body. Perhaps one day a film would be made about my experiences!

But the glow soon turned into a chill as I began to ponder on what could really happen when I arrived at the customs at Havana Airport. It was as if God were saying, 'Peter, you'll never do it. Those guards are too clever. They'll find everything you have.'

I realised that all the skill in the world didn't matter. Those guards were highly trained to sniff out any literature that was not wanted in Cuba.

'My God,' I prayed 'I am so sorry. I got carried away in the excitement of the moment. I now realise that I can go only in your strength, not mine. This isn't a game, it's for real.'

I jumped out of bed, switched on the light, and tumbled all the contents of the case onto the floor.

'Hey, Peter, what's going on?' asked Blanca, her voice blurred, still half asleep.

'I'm going to repack the case. James Bond was wrong. God was right.'

I put all my clothes in the bottom of the case and all the books and Bibles on top. Those that wouldn't fit went into my briefcase.

'Chiquita,' I declared, 'I want us to walk in one hundred per cent dependence on God. So I am not going to be clever any more. We will never get these things in, but He can.'

*   *   *

The sky had turned an ugly plum colour as a tropical storm swept over Havana. Our little plane touched down at the airport just as the storm reached its height.

Blanca and I made a dash for the waiting bus that would take us into the terminal, but we still got soaked.

'Well, Chiquita, this is it.'

She didn't speak. I could read the tension in her face.

'We are going to be all right, aren't we, Peter?'

I nodded, but when I saw the sombre-faced customs officials waiting inside, I began to feel panic-stricken.

'Chiquita, it's going to take a miracle to get anything through that lot.'

She squeezed my hand.

'Let's silently pray the "smuggler's prayer" that Brother Andrew used in his book when he was taking God's Word into Eastern Europe.'

Before I could offer my prayer, I saw our bags appear. They were the first off the carousel.

'Chiquita,' I whispered, 'let's stay back a little and watch the others go through. Then we can see how they are searching the baggage.'

Even as I spoke, a customs man hovered close by. I accidentally caught his eye, and he spotted the bags. He beckoned me to bring them to his table.

This was it! There was no way out now.

We stood at his table. I remembered the prayer I was going to recite, and silently repeated it:

'Lord, in my luggage I have Scriptures that I want to take to your children across this border. When you were on earth, you made blind eyes see. Now, I pray, make seeing eyes blind. Do not let the guards see those things you do not want them to see.'

The official, who was obviously a senior officer, signalled to a woman to begin the search.

'Your customs declaration form,' she snapped.

'I'm sorry, I don't have one.'

She handed me a form. 'Fill it in now. I will watch.'

'But what do I write?'

She was now growing impatient.

'You put down everything you are bringing into the country.'

'Everything? Like what?'

'Like your camera, and your watch.' I filled in those items.

'Do you have an electric shaver?'

'No, officer, I don't.'

'What else do you have?'

'Well, just some personal belongings.' I reasoned that the books were personal because I had bought them.

She scanned the sheet of paper and then said, 'Right open up your cases.'

My heart fluttered frantically.

'Oh God, now you have to act!' I shot up a telegram prayer. 'Otherwise I'm in big trouble and your children won't get these precious books and Bibles.'

As I began to unzip one of our cases, she said, 'No, start with your briefcase.'

That was just as bad. It was also full of Bibles.

I opened it and there, exposed, were those beautiful leather-bound Bibles. She must have seen them.

I looked at her peering down at them, then almost involuntarily said, 'Hey, officer, I have a confession to make.'

She looked startled.

'Yes, I have brought with me a little battery-operated electric shaver. I'm sorry. When you asked me if I had one I said "no". And I forgot to put it on the form.'

With that I pulled it from the briefcase and handed it to her.

'Please take it. I would like you to have it.'

I could see some of her hardness, some of that exterior shell, begin to crack.

'Sir, I have no need for a razor.' With that, she carefully placed it back on top of the Bibles.

Without further ado, she stamped my declaration form and said, 'O.K., you can go. Enjoy your stay in Cuba.'

Blanca and I hardly dared breathe as we made our way out of the terminal lugging our precious (and heavy) cargo.

That night, in our Havana hotel room, I began searching through the telephone directory for the telephone numbers of churches. I had memorised some addresses, but my instructions were to find new contacts. I noticed with surprise that several churches were listed.

I dialled one and managed to get the pastor on the line.

'I am a Mexican Christian visiting Cuba and I would like to see you,' I told him.

'I'm sorry, my friend, I cannot see you.' I could hear the fear in the man's voice vibrating down the line.

He did give me the number of a man he said was a 'high-up official in the Ecumenical Council of Cuba'. That man was most friendly and said he would come to see me next morning.

The well-dressed official shook hands with Blanca and me and asked us if we would like to see some of the sights of the Cuban capital.

As we drove around the city in his car, I noted how this former playground for Americans now looked very down-at-heel. As the city flashed by, our host answered my questions about the Christian Church in Cuba.

'No, we don't have any problems at all . . . we don't need any more Bibles . . . I personally have three myself . . . Christian books? We have plenty.'

I was shocked. I had been told that life was hard for believers on the island, yet this man, who should know, was telling me that all my preconceived ideas were wrong.

That afternoon's organised tour was agony for me. I kept wondering what I was doing in Cuba. If the Ecumenical Council man was telling the truth, we had gone through the tension of the customs for nothing.

I lay on my bed that night feeling very uneasy. Surely all those people who had briefed me before I left could not have been so wrong?

Then I remembered the name and phone number of a family who lived in the interior. It had been impressed upon me when I was about to leave.

'Just call them, mention my name, and tell them that you are in Havana. The pastor will come to see you,' my contact had told me.

I recalled the last words of my instructions.

'From him you will learn the real story.'

So I called and left a message saying which hotel I was in.

151

The next morning Blanca and I went down early for breakfast. As we stepped out of the elevator, I saw dozens of people milling around in the lobby. But there, sitting straight in front of me, was a middle-aged man with a soft round face.

'Lord, is that him?' I asked.

I had the distinct impression it was. He looked so peaceful, yet alive, compared with the other people who often seemed to have zombie-like expressions.

He responded to my glance with a wave. I strode purposefully over and hugged him tightly. We both kept repeating, 'God bless you, brother. God bless you, brother.'

I finally managed to disentangle myself from this brother and introduce my wife. He shook her hand warmly, and said, 'I am Pastor Arturo Flores. I have come a long way to see you.'

I later realised that, even in coming into the hotel as he did, he had taken a great risk. In his position, he should not have been fraternising with foreigners. I asked him how he had managed to get here so early.

'Oh, brother, as soon as I heard you were here I dropped everything I was doing to get on an all-night bus,' he explained. 'Years have passed since I last had a relationship with anyone from outside the island. I wanted to talk to you to find out how the Body of Christ is doing in the free world.'

Since he hadn't eaten I invited him to join us in the hotel cafeteria, which was normally reserved for guests and not Cubans. Afterwards I dashed up to my room to collect my canvas souvenir bag, having told the pastor to wait for me outside the hotel.

We walked a few blocks together, and the pastor suddenly put his hand on my arm. 'Brother, do you have a Bible?'

My face didn't react at all.

'A Bible? Why do you need a Bible? We were told that there are many Bibles on the island; that there is no need for them.'

'Who told you that?'

I recounted my conversation with the official from the Ecumenical Council of Cuba.

'Brother, let me tell you that over the past twenty years only about 15,000 Bibles have been allowed in here for a population of ten million!'

He paused to let his words sink in. 'Barely one in three or four believers in Cuba have Bibles, and many of those are so old that they are literally falling apart from use. We desperately need new Bibles.' Then he added, 'Brother, you have to realise that in Cuba there are two factions. There are those who belong to the government-sponsored Ecumenical Council and those, including my group of churches, who will have nothing to do with them.'

'But why?'

'Because they are hand-in-glove with the atheist government. How can light walk with darkness?'

I asked him if there were many Christian groups in Cuba who had not become part of the official organisation.

'Brother, we are in the majority. We will not compromise our faith for anyone. We want to be free to worship and teach without compromising our message. We don't want anyone to dictate to us what we preach.'

Coming, as I did, from a free society, I didn't completely understand all that he was saying. But he certainly painted a different picture from my first contact in Cuba.

But then he returned to his original question.

'Brother Peter, you remember I asked you a few minutes ago if you had a Bible?'

I looked serious.

'I'm afraid I haven't got *a* Bible.'

His face dropped.

'But, brother, I thought that because you have come from a country where Bibles are freely available, you would have brought one.'

He confessed that he had given his last Bible away to a couple he had recently married.

I pulled him into an alleyway and whispered in his ear. 'Brother, I do not have *a* Bible – I have *many* Bibles. Look.'

His eyes widened when he saw inside my bag.

He lovingly took out one of the Bibles bound in black leather and handled it like the most precious thing he had seen in his life.

'Is this for me?'

'Yes, brother, not only that one, but also this one . . . and this one . . .' I eventually placed ten Bibles in his hands.

He burst into laughter and then tears began to trickle down his cheeks. They were tears of joy.

I handed over the whole bag to him. 'Take it, pastor. Take everything I have brought.'

Then, as I looked at his simple clothes, I told him that I had also brought in some clothing. 'I want you to have all of those as well,' I told him. We met again several times so that I could fill the plastic bags he brought with more clothing.

At our last meeting the pastor said, 'Be sure you tell my friends in America that we have new benches in our little church. We did it for the glory of God in our spare time.'

His face glowed with pride.

'We will certainly do that, brother.'

After making several other fruitful contacts on that first trip behind the 'Sugarcane Curtain,' we at last returned home.

I went over in my mind all that had happened. Pastor Flores's beaming face kept recurring. He had been so proud of the rough wooden benches he had helped to make. I thought of how we, in the so-called free world, have so much freedom, so many material advantages, yet I had never met anyone like him before in my travels. He was so thrilled with the little things he had. I had never seen a pastor in the West handle a Bible with such love and concern as this Cuban pastor.

'Oh God,' I prayed as we flew over the blue Caribbean waters, 'help us never to take anything for granted. Help us to appreciate all that we have and take full advantage of it. And Lord, continue to be with our brothers and sisters in Cuba. May they teach us many lessons . . .'

20. 'More than Conquerors'

Brother Andrew showed intense interest as our car passed close to the tiered parapets of El Morro, the famous Puerto Rican fort, in the centre of old San Juan. This formidable construction had once seen much bloody fighting as the powers of another age fought for control of this charming, sun-drenched island.

The car juddered over the cobblestone paving as we admired patios and courtyards, overhanging balconies, and the religious shrines of San Juan.

My companions on this journey were Andrew, his right-hand man, John and Dale Kietzman. We were heading towards '*Catacomba* Cathedral 1' on the edge of the capital city.

'You know, friends,' said Brother Andrew, his features taut, 'I haven't preached in too many cathedrals before. This is going to be a new experience for me.'

I smiled.

'Andrew, I understand this is just the first of a group of these 'cathedrals' spread across the island. Pedro, the founder, is a former drug addict and hippie. He is an extraordinary character.'

After twenty minutes we came to a small wood with a sign which pointed to the 'cathedral'.

'This is certainly a strange place for a cathedral,' observed John, a tall, blond, well-built Dutchman.

Our driver eased the vehicle along a narrow dusty pathway. As I wound down my window, I could hear the sound of singing wafting in from the woods. It was accompanied by maracas, tambourines and guitars.

Brother Andrew caught his breath with surprise when he eventually caught sight of the large crowd of young people. The worshippers were mostly dressed in casual clothes and many had their hands raised towards the branches of the trees that partly covered their meeting place.

Bemused, we got out of the car and extended our hands to the exuberant group that immediately surrounded us.

'Welcome to our "cathedral",' said Pedro, a small man with features that looked as though they had been chiselled out of granite.

His brown eyes sparkled as he asked, 'Brother Andrew, I guess this must be the most unusual cathedral you've ever been to?'

The Dutchman nodded.

'Do you like our decorations?' asked Pedro, pointing to the Bible verses that had been inscribed on some of the trees and also on large stones scattered around the open-air sanctuary.

'Most unusual,' muttered Brother Andrew, shaking his head in disbelief.

Pedro then pointed to the stumps of trees and lengths of logs that were scattered around the open-air church.

'These are our seats,' he said, grinning broadly. 'They may not be as comfortable as those in normal cathedrals, but they are fine for us. You know, Brother Andrew, we don't believe in expensive buildings. We know that Jesus is coming back soon and we don't have the time to put them up. We need to use our time to tell others in our country about Jesus.'

Pedro could see the look of interest on our faces, so he continued.

'We began our movement back in 1971, shortly after I had become a Christian. Before that I was taking L.S.D. and hashish. My life was a real mess. I found that many churches in my country didn't seem too interested in drop-outs like me. Soon many others, mostly hippies, also came to know the Lord and we began meeting in what we eventually called a *Catacomba*. We now have eighteen of these groups meeting in the open air around the island.'

We were puzzled by the *Catacombas*.

'Oh,' said Pedro, 'that's easy to explain. I had been reading a book about the Christians martyred in Rome, and realised that one day we, too, could be called on to suffer and lay down our lives for Christ. This book spoke about Rome's catacombs, the subterranean vaults and passages used by the early Christians as a place of refuge during times of persecution. We decided that one day we might also have to seek refuge as they did. So we have become *Catacombas* – underground Christians.'

As we talked above the singing, Pedro introduced us to Manuel, another young *Catacomba*. After shaking hands he produced from the boot of his car a map which he unrolled in front of us.

'This,' Manuel explained, 'is a map of the drain system of San Juan. If persecution comes we can literally go underground immediately, just like the early Christians in Rome.'

I whistled in disbelief.

'We already have haversacks, sleeping bags, torches . . . we are prepared to become invisible either in the drains or in the mountains. We even know of caves where we can hide Bibles.'

'But,' interrupted John, 'many believers in this part of the world tell us that persecution will never happen here. What makes you so sure it will?'

'We have already seen what has happened to Cuba,' Pedro told me, conviction ringing in his voice. 'Now Nicaragua has had its revolution and El Salvador is in the middle of one. We can see all these troubles creeping slowly towards Puerto Rico. That's why we must prepare. We are willing to pay any price to keep our liberty as Christians. We know that persecution can come from either the left or the right.'

His face became very serious.

'My friends,' he said, 'we are willing to be martyrs if God calls on us to be.'

Brother Andrew was impressed and put his arm around

Pedro's shoulder. The two felt a real kinship.

Our little party then followed the wiry leader to the front of the 'cathedral' and after a few more minutes of singing, we were introduced to the young worshippers.

I translated into Spanish as Brother Andrew began to talk to them in the chatty style that has had such an impact on Christians around the world. The Dutch smuggler recounts stories in a way that forces people to the edge of their seats, or in this case, their tree stumps.

As he spoke, the sun slowly turned to blood-orange, then sank behind the trees. Paraffin pressure-lamps were lit, as Andrew began the story of the missionary whom he admires more than any other, C. T. Studd, the former English international cricketer and founder of the World-wide Evangelization Crusade.

'Studd had been a member of the "Cambridge Seven" who went out from England to form a strong evangelism team to work with Hudson Taylor in China,' he told the audience. 'He had been a very wealthy man, but gave up everything for Jesus. The Lord used him greatly in China.'

Brother Andrew told the eager group that this former cricketer, because of his relentless labour and sacrificial living, became seriously ill.

'He was so sick that the doctors called him a "museum of tropical diseases",' he said.

'One day he was walking in town and saw an announcement for a missionary rally. The notice read, "Cannibals Need Missionaries".'

This provoked broad smiles all around.

'Studd went to the rally and there God called him to be a missionary to Africa. He was already a grandfather and still a desperately sick man but he went to the heart of Africa, where no missionary had ever been. He worked day and night to give the native people the Gospel. During the seventeen pain-racked years he worked in Africa he did not go home on furlough once. Throughout those years he saw his wife, Priscilla, only one time. He loved her and his children but he wanted them to be in Britain to organise the home front – the prayer force.'

There was by now rapt attention on every face.

'I have talked to a number of people who worked with Studd in Africa and I have heard some amazing stories about the man. Such an inspiring life!

'He was always looking for people who could take over from him but he was a hard master. He had forsaken everything for the Lord and he demanded the same of his followers. He had a right to do that. You cannot ask anyone to do that which you have not done yourself, but he had done it all.'

Brother Andrew's blue eyes by now blazed.

'Because of the pain he was experiencing near the end, C. T. Studd often had to be given pain-killing drugs to help him continue. His personal attendant, Jimmy Taylor, a Baptist, was there with him. One night, he thought that Studd was definitely dying so he went over at eleven p.m. to give him an injection to kill the pain. When he left, the great missionary was asleep.

'At about three a.m., Taylor became concerned again and thought that he had better go and check to see if Studd was still alive. When he arrived at the hut where the missionary leader lived, he was shocked to find the bed empty,' Brother Andrew's eyes twinkled with anticipation.

'On the table were pages with writing on and a little note which read: "Dear Jim, I have translated a couple more chapters of Acts and now I am off on my bicycle to reach another tribe for Jesus. They have never heard of Him".'

Soft chuckling broke out as Brother Andrew explained that this was just hours after he had been given his 'last' shot.

'Nobody could follow C. T. Studd,' the Dutchman said earnestly. 'His steps were far too big. He really had no followers. Almost all of his co-workers left him in despair because they couldn't keep up with him.

'Shortly before his death, he called in his daughter, who had come to visit him in Africa, and said that he would like to give her something in memory of her father. He looked around his hut, trying to find something for her, and then said, "I have nothing left. I have given everything to Jesus".'

Brother Andrew cleared his throat and then asked, 'Can we say that?'

Brother Andrew paused to let his words take effect, then added, 'I know that many of you here tonight are willing to lay down your lives for Christ, just like C. T. Studd. That is wonderful. But are you also willing to be a servant? Are you willing to serve each other? Are you willing to be what I call a "dirty-jobs" Christian?'

The sky overhead was now speckled with bright stars as heads bobbed, and voices whispered back, 'Yes!'

* * *

'There's trouble everywhere, Brother Andrew,' the Guatemalan pastor said as we sat in our hotel room in the capital, Guatemala City.

'It is especially rife among the young people, the students. Some students recently suspected the government of planting spies on campus to see what they were up to. When they discovered one of them they took him out into the open and burned him alive. It was terrible.'

The pastor then told us about happenings in the Quiche region of the country.

'The believers there are being persecuted by both the right and the left. The rightists accuse them of being leftists and vice versa. They don't want to be involved in politics, but just want to be able to worship God in freedom. By now many churches have closed and the pastors have fled from the region. We know that soon the same troubles are going to come to us here in the capital city.'

He turned to our little group. 'Brothers, what can you do to help us?'

We felt that one of the most important things we could offer was an opportunity for the pastors to prepare specifically for persecution. The 'Victory Seminar' had already been used successfully by Open Doors in South-East Asia and, with some adaptation, could have some excellent lessons for Latin America. The teaching would centre on what the Bible had to say about persecution, and on the importance of discipleship and fellowship.

The pastor was thrilled at such a prospect. I stressed that our concern was not simply for material survival, but for victorious Christian living in every situation, no matter how difficult.

I rejoiced that the work of Open Doors was meeting a real need.

The next stop on our eventful Central American trip was El Salvador, blood-soaked after a recent military coup.

Andrew was anxious to meet Christians in the capital of San Salvador and was disturbed to find that none of them seemed to take seriously the implications of the turmoil in their country. We were struck by the irony of its being the only land in the world named after 'The Saviour'.

'Brother Andrew,' said one pastor, 'we know El Salvador well. Better than you. There will be no persecution of believers here. It will never happen here.'

Our group looked at each other blankly. I could see that Brother Andrew was concerned with their apparent smugness.

That evening, the newspapers carried a terrifying headline *Estado de Sitio* (State of Siege).

I read aloud to Andrew and John the news that the military had, that very day, introduced a six p.m. curfew. 'Anyone caught on the streets after that time could be shot,' I told them. 'Apparently the new government has abandoned all civil rights.'

That afternoon we took a taxi ride around San Salvador. The taxi driver often had his foot to the floor as the cab screeched around the streets: he didn't want to get caught up in trouble.

'Hey, did you hear about the massacre on that corner earlier today?' he asked as we hurtled around one bend in the road.

We shook our heads.

'The National Guard went in and killed a lot of students for demonstrating. We are on the verge of civil war. It looks as though what happened in Nicaragua could happen here.'

Next morning, a small group of ashen-faced pastors arrived at the hotel to meet us again. This time only six showed up.

'Brothers,' said their spokesman, his voice sinking to a whisper, 'we have an apology to make to you. First of all, our other brothers haven't come because they feel the streets are too dangerous for them to be out. And secondly, we were wrong. We said that persecution could never happen here. We can at last see the warning signs.'

There was an awkward pause, then he added: 'What can you do to help us? We really do want to be more than conquerors!'

21. The Third Option

Maria's baby looked up at me and gurgled.

My youngest sister Maria, a trained nurse, had popped around to see us from her nearby home. Both she and her husband, Jaime, a Mexican-American, had been living in California for one year.

'He is so beautiful,' I told her.

My three sons, Azael, Eduardo and Ali, crowded around to watch him kick his legs in the air.

Nellie, our eldest daughter, would have been with us if it wasn't for her new secretarial job.

Settling down with cups of tea, we were soon chatting about the latest family news. Maria hadn't been home for a year, and since I had just come from seeing my parents in Mexico City she was anxious to learn how they were.

'Papa has had a successful operation on his eye,' I told her.

Her face creased into a smile.

'He can see better than ever before,' I went on. 'You know, before the operation, he was almost totally blind. Now he's like a young kid again. And you know that Nellie is following the family tradition?'

'What do you mean?'

'She's battling for the underdog. Our sister is now the representative to the city council. She takes up any problem the residents raise with the council. They say she is a tough person to deal with.'

Maria laughed. 'What a family we have, brother.'

I nodded. 'But that's not all. Rosa has been involved in

the women's liberation movement. For a while she was a real activist. Now she's cooled off a bit, and become a music teacher for the kids of her community. She plays the organ in church and conducts the choir, and now feels that it's more important for her to win these children for Christ through music than to be out on the streets protesting.'

Maria was particularly interested in Ruben. 'The last I heard he was going out into the countryside trying to organise co-operatives for the artisans. Is he still doing that?'

'Yes, but he's getting into trouble out in some of the villages. He told me last time I saw him about starting a co-operative in Tiapujalpa. It is still functioning now, but it almost cost Ruben his life.'

I repeated the story to Maria. Ruben had been taken to the village by a truck from the Department of Industry and Commerce, but at first he was unable to find anyone willing to come to a meeting to hear about his plan. Then, to make matters worse, he was suddenly surrounded by a crowd drunk on *pulque* (the popular intoxicating home brew of the Aztecs). Ruben tried to explain what he was doing, but they said they had been given promises before by the electricity company which had come to nothing. So anyone representing the government was no longer believed.

Suddenly, one of the drunkards lashed at him with a machete. Fortunately, Ruben avoided the blow but it was only when he agreed to join them in drinking *pulque* that they began to take notice of what he wanted to share. In the end they liked his proposals and, after a round of hand-shakes, signed a document he drew up. Many had to sign with their thumb-prints.

Ruben had now organised more than fifty-six co-operatives around the country.

The conversation turned to Cesar, who was planning to move to Nicaragua. He had presented a plan to the Sandinista government for an effective literacy campaign, and although many others had submitted different ideas Cesar's plan was chosen. He was moving to Managua to be chief adviser to the project.

Maria looked worried for a moment, concerned for Cesar's safety, then asked after Olivia.

'She is hard at work as well,' I told her. 'She has written two books about fighting injustice in Latin America, and is now working on her third. I haven't read them yet, but I understand some evangelicals find them very radical.'

'And what about you?' Maria asked gently. 'You are dashing all over this troubled continent of ours. Are you seeing things to encourage you now?'

I told her that I was more and more convinced that a change of heart through Christ was the only way to justice and peace.

'Everyone needs *this* revolution, and no one more than those in the established Church. The persecution of Protestants by Catholics is terrible. I heard of a case in Puebla recently of a young couple who had lost their baby but were denied permission to bury their son because he was not Catholic. They had to take their case to the police authorities, and finally buried the child under police protection. Christians here are in such a difficult position,' I told her. These things were so close to my heart that my response to Maria's question just flowed on.

'Recently, in El Salvador, the junta called a group of Christian leaders together and asked them which side they were on. Did they support the right or the left? Their answer was, "We do not believe we should take a political position. Our mission is to work for peace and justice so that God can help to solve the problems as soon as possible. We are also called to pray for those who are in authority over us, and we ask our people to do that regularly."

'So the junta asked them, "Well, why not pray for us right now, that we will be the ones to bring peace and justice?" The pastors did pray with these government officials for peace and justice in their country. The press was there and the next day the newspapers carried a big story with pictures claiming that the Christian leaders were praying for the government. The guerrillas read this distortion and decided that the Christians were, in fact, on the side of the government. Now several of the pastors have had to leave the country because they have received anonymous threats on their lives.'

Maria was nodding in agreement. 'Profound change is needed, you are right,' she said softly. 'Violence is not the answer. You must keep going on the "royal pathway" as Mama would say, and tell people of Christ's alternative.'

'Mama misses us, you know, now that we are all away.' I remembered thinking what a lonely figure she seemed when I was last home. 'But she wouldn't have any of us change course – she's proud of what we're doing.'

'You know, Peter, from what you've told me I think we could do with a few more "royal" people in Latin America.'

22. 'New Men' in Nicaragua

'Peter.' Brother Andrew leaned forward in his chair. 'When are we going to be able to meet your brother Cesar?'

I was now with Andrew and John in post-revolutionary Nicaragua, and had told them about Cesar and his incredible literacy crusade.

'It is difficult, Andrew,' I said. 'Cesar is very busy with the programme. But he did promise me on the phone a few minutes ago that he would come and spend some time with us this afternoon.'

When he arrived, Cesar's deep brown eyes were shining as we gave each other an *abrazo*.

'It's so good to see you again, brother,' I said as his huge black beard tickled my face. 'I hardly recognise you under so much hair.'

'Peter,' he chuckled, 'you must grow one. It's the thing to do now in Latin America.'

I laughed and then led him over to Brother Andrew and John. He shook hands with them warmly.

'My friends, welcome to my country.'

I was puzzled. 'But Cesar, I thought we were Mexicans!'

'Peter,' his eyes were bright with enthusiasm, 'when you start caring about people every frontier disappears. I feel as Nicaraguan as the Nicaraguans.'

I knew what he meant. In a similar way, I felt a citizen of Latin America, and no longer just Mexican.

Coffee was ordered. I was longing to know more specifically how Cesar came to offer his plan for a literacy campaign to the Sandinistas.

167

'When the revolution was going on here,' he told us,' I was happy to watch it from the safety of the seminary. I enjoyed being a professor there, but the great needs in Nicaragua still impressed themselves upon me, even more so when the revolution was over. Out of the blue I was asked by Fernando Cardenal, a Jesuit priest who had been nominated National Co-ordinator for this new literacy crusade, whether I had any ideas to put forward. Then, as you know, my plan was the one accepted.'

'Didn't you want to go to Mexico City for your sabbatical?' I asked, knowing that was to have been the next step.

'Peter, when I saw the ravages of the war here, and the level of illiteracy, I simply couldn't turn my back on the situation. I wanted to make my contribution to the history of the revolution. I felt my commitment to these people as a Christian, and as a Latin.'

I turned to get Brother Andrew's and John's reactions. Their eyes were fixed on his face. Like myself, they could not but admire Cesar's sincerity. His empathy with the Nicaraguan people was obvious for all to see.

My brother went on to explain how, in his master plan, he had aimed to train a huge number of Nicaraguans to go out into all parts of the country to train others in their turn.

'We brought together a small group and taught them with audio-visual aids, posters, movies, etc. and then trained them to use these tools to teach others. Soon they were fanning out all over the place, until 180,000 people were trained.'

'But Cesar, that's an enormous number!' I gasped.

'Peter, the plan was for those 180,000 to teach simple reading and writing to 800,000 Nicaraguans in less than one year.'

He paused to allow his words to sink in.

'We *will* succeed. Already our country has been turned into one big school. Everyone is learning from others. The trainers are sent into the countryside to live with the families there. They have no salary, but they have to live in, say, with a farmer and his family.

'So the trainer goes out with the farmer and milks the cows with him. He then teaches him how to write "milk" and "cow". It is a practical training. And the trainer benefits too by learning about a completely new way of life. It's really exciting.'

Brother Andrew was fascinated.

'What have the trainers learned about life in the rural areas since they have been there?' he asked.

Cesar's face clouded.

'They found many bad things. That town after town had no school, hospital or even a doctor. The people had been living without any social benefits and without education. Do you know, Brother Andrew, we found that there were whole towns where not one person knew how to read and write. In fact, in most of them some 90 per cent of the people were illiterate.'

'But why would Somoza keep the people in such a state?' I questioned. 'It doesn't make sense.'

'That's easy, Peter. If the people remained ignorant they wouldn't question what was happening. That way, Somoza could keep an iron grip on everything.'

A flush of anger darkened his face.

'You know, our trainers found whole communities where just about all the people suffered from tuberculosis. People couldn't even remember seeing a doctor in the area. Not one doctor in their lifetime!'

I could understand his feelings. Cesar's voice rose as he continued:

'Our people are now piecing together the true story of Nicaragua. It's being written for the first time. There is a special brigade with hundreds of cassette recorders taping people's experiences. They are coming up with stories of the anonymous heroes who died fighting the hated dictator. We are learning of towns where only about ten freedom fighters survived out of three hundred.'

As he paused for breath, I jumped in with a question that was burning in my mind.

'Cesar, what about the spiritual side? Have Christians here been able to use the literacy crusade to communicate their faith?'

He scratched his head, as if embarrassed.

'Brother, there was some discussion about whether or not Christians should use the crusade to propagate the Gospel. One problem was that if we allowed one group to do it, we would also have to allow those who have deviated from what I consider to be the truth.'

'Like whom?' I asked.

'Like the Mormons and the Jehovah's Witnesses. So we made a rule that no one within the literary crusade could use it as a platform to proselytise. But outside class hours, they could share their faith as they wanted to.'

I nodded. 'What about you, Cesar? How have you communicated the faith which you accepted?' A look of sadness spread across his face as he answered.

'Well, my dear brother, I want to tell you that I found that there is a time to talk and a time to stay quiet. We read about that in the book of Ecclesiastes. So there is a time to preach the Word, and there is a time when you preach with your life.'

There was, by now, a slight edge to his voice.

'Everybody here knows that I am an evangelical Christian. They don't reject me. They accept my way of thinking and being, knowing that I'm a sincere believer. They know I am doing all this for Him. They see me working late hours with them all the time, not for myself, but for Christ. I don't preach to them but they can see that I'm standing for the eternal values of the Gospel.'

With that, Cesar consulted his watch.

'Look, my friends, it has been a privilege to meet you, but now I have to go. I'm leaving this evening with a brigade to the interior. I want to see how things are going.'

I walked with Cesar to the car park.

I took his arm and said, 'Cesar, I admire all that you are doing here, but you look so tired. When will you stop and rest? You can't go on like this for ever.'

He read the concern in my eyes.

'Peter, I have to go on. So many people are learning to read and write, and I have been asked to stay on to advise about further education in the country. I'll stay here until we have been able to create a completely *new man* in Nicaragua.'

With that he slid into the driver's seat of his modest little car and turned on the ignition. The engine roared into life and he drove away.

I went back to the coffee shop and recounted the final conversation with Andrew and John.

Andrew's face lit up. 'Cesar wants to create a completely *new man* in this country, and we should help him. We know that only God can make a man completely new, so we, in Open Doors, should help provide the Word of God to those who are learning to read and write. Then there will be many *new people* all over Nicaragua. Jesus will have made them new through His Word!'

23. Revolutions in the Land of the Smoking Gun

'You have to be either crazy or very brave.'

The grim-faced driver raised one damp finger in the air as he spoke.

'Don't you know that many people were killed just a few days ago in the very *barrio* you want to go to? The National Guard went in to kill as many guerrillas as they could. The place is full of terrorists.'

I shouldn't have been surprised with the man's comments. I was back in San Salvador, capital of violence-torn El Salvador, dubbed by the world's media as 'The land of the smoking gun'. With me were Adalid Silva, a Nicaraguan-born pastor who has a successful young people's ministry across Central America, and my British co-author, Dan Wooding.

The troubles in El Salvador had by now (1981) reached apalling proportions. Official figures in San Salvador showed that during the previous eighteen months of the so-called 'centralist junta', 30,000 people had been killed in the violence.

The traffic in the capital city demonstrated the general nervousness. Red traffic lights were hardly adhered to. No one wanted to risk being shot by a guerrilla while waiting to move off, and then being burnt to cinders when the car was 'fired'. Our taxi driver had agreed to take us to our destination only after haggling for a good price.

'Are you journalists?' he questioned us roughly as we bumped along. 'Only journalists come here now.'

I explained that we were Christians, and had been

172

invited to the *barrio* to speak and share our faith. 'We want to tell the young men and women that there is hope.'

The cab driver looked disbelieving, but then his expression relaxed. 'I have to tell you something. I am a Catholic and each day I put my life in the hands of God. I don't practise my religion as I should, but I do know that the only hope for our country now is God.'

Suddenly he screeched to a halt. He had driven around the *barrio* for five minutes trying to find the address we had given him.

'It's not safe for me to stay here any longer. Please get out and ask someone for your friend's home.'

'But –'

'Please give me the money and go,' he interrupted. The man was trembling all over.

We did as he asked and began walking down an alleyway in the *barrio*. As we did so, I felt my heart start pounding. I looked at the Nicaraguan. He had a camera with a large telephoto lens on it.

'Brother, that could be dangerous,' I told him. 'Someone could think you are carrying a bazooka and shoot you; in fact, blast all of us.'

Then I turned to my ruddy-faced British friend. He also had a camera around his neck and was carrying a large red bag that, to a suspicious person, could appear to contain a machine gun. Even worse than that, his Anglo-Saxon features made him a sitting target for any sniper. We were so vulnerable. This was absurdly dangerous and I knew it. As we walked I felt fear churning in my stomach. I sent up one of my telegram prayers, 'Lord, please let us find this address as soon as possible.'

During our nerve-shattering walk through these alleys, I noticed many eyes peering out through windows at us. Finally, I found the house and knocked urgently at the door. There was no reply. So I shouted through the letter box, 'Is there anyone in?'

Still no reply. But then, without warning, the door of a neighbouring house was flung open and a woman stood there.

'Yes.'

I explained that we were looking for the young pastor of the house church in the area.

'Oh, you've come to the wrong place,' she said, her tone now more friendly. 'He does live there, but he asked me to tell you that the meeting you've come for is three blocks away – back there.' She pointed down the threatening alleys we had just walked through.

My heart began to pound again.

'Does that mean we have to go all the way back through there?' Dan asked incredulously.

'I'm afraid so, brother. Let's just claim God's protection for this walk.'

A young boy was assigned by the woman to be our guide and we stepped out at a brisk pace until, after twelve nerve-racking minutes, we finally came to the bungalow where the meeting was to be held. A few swarthy young people milled around the alley. They looked around in astonishment as they spotted us.

Arturo, the pastor, only twenty years of age, greeted us warmly as we stepped into a long room filled with trestle tables. Inside, three or four women, helped by some girls, were preparing a meal.

'It is Mother's Day,' explained the fresh-faced pastor. 'We are having a celebration and inviting the young people of the area to come and join us.'

Even as he spoke, the room became grave-quiet. It seemed that the Englishman's non-Latin features were the problem. All conversation stopped. Obviously the women felt that Dan's presence could put all of them in danger. The silence seemed interminable.

'Is this a funeral?' Adalid admonished everyone at last. 'Look, our friend has come all the way from England. Don't look so glum. Jesus is here and He will protect us.' His forceful tone rebuked those present.

Slowly a trickle of teenage boys and girls came in and were soon scattered about the room.

The pastor came over and whispered in my ear, 'Peter, there could be real trouble here today. Some of the young people who are coming in could be guerrillas!'

As he spoke, I felt an almost ungovernable urge to get up and leave. Just as I was doing battle in my mind, one of these 'guerrillas' came and sat opposite me. His sunken eyes seemed to hold all the miserable secrets of a nightmare.

'I've just come out of prison,' he told me. 'I was accused of being a terrorist, but I wouldn't admit anything. I was tortured for thirteen days. It was terrible.'

Then he gave a wry smile.

'I've just been here a few minutes and already I can feel the love in this place.'

As we sat and looked at each other, I began to pray silently, 'Lord, you know how scared I feel at this time, but I don't want to feel like that. I want to know your peace. Help me to love these young people right now.'

At once I felt a deep warmth flood my body.

More and more teenagers shuffled into the meeting.

I began talking to another youth, his face looking grim and determined.

'You know, my friend,' he told me in a confidential tone, 'if you think things are bad now in our country, I can tell you that they are going to get even worse.'

Soon the room was packed to the doors. We all tucked into a delicious plate of meat and rice, with a spicy sauce. When it was all over the young pastor told everyone to move the tables to the side and then invited Dan to speak.

I had to swallow my fear and get up with Dan to translate his words into Spanish. Dan simply told how as a teenager he had been a rebel in his home town of Birmingham, England, and had eventually left home to live in Toronto, Canada.

The room went quiet as he said, 'I was full of hatred for the whole world. But eventually I realised how terrible hate can be and, through a serious illness that came to my father, I swallowed my pride, went back home, and accepted Christ into my life.

'With that, all my anger went and was replaced with love. I know that many of you here today have hate in your heart.

But Jesus can take that away and replace it with a revolution of love.'

I noticed the trickle of a tear appearing on the tanned cheek of a young man near the front.

Now came my turn to speak. What could I say to such a group? What was the answer to their problems?

I turned and looked at them. All eyes were fixed on my face.

'What is it you most want here in El Salvador?' I asked them. 'Is it liberty and freedom?'

I then referred them to the 'Mariel boat people' who had left Cuba in 1980 for a better life in the United States.

'When they arrived on the Florida coast they found the material things they had dreamed about in their new life were not waiting for them. They discovered they would have to struggle for them. They had to fight for their food, their clothing, their housing. Many of them found that they were not welcome in their new land.

'We made many contacts with them in Miami, where they faced new problems. It was then I realised that liberty does not come from material things, the sort of things many of them wanted. It comes from inside the heart. It's created from the soul. You can have all the freedom you need, all the money you need, a beautiful house and a shiny new car, but then you may become the slave of an incurable sickness, of the fear that someone is going to take it all away from you. Or you can have the freedom to do whatever you want without anyone dictating to you what to do. But still you then become a slave of sin.'

I then recounted the story of a good friend of mine who lived in a 'free country'.

'He lives in a fine democracy, but he had been a slave to leprosy, and had to live in a leper colony. One day someone came and shared with him the spiritual liberty that Jesus can give. And he accepted it.

'His situation didn't change; certainly not at first, anyway. He still had to live in the leprosarium, but his soul and his mind were cleansed and changed. Inside, he became a different person. Later on, in a special service, he was totally healed of his leprosy. He was finally free of his illness, but more important, his soul and mind are totally free.'

Then I turned the pages of my Bible to Luke 5:12 and 13, and read to them, 'While he was in one of the cities, there came a man full of leprosy, and when he saw Jesus, he fell on his face and besought him, "Lord, if you will, you can make me clean." And he stretched out his hand, and touched him, saying, "I will; be clean." And immediately the leprosy left him.'

I again looked at the group, not knowing what atrocities some of them had been involved in. 'I know this afternoon that many of you feel loaded with pain, hatred, and anguish, because you see the injustice and the poverty here; you feel that you cannot change the situation in your country. You want not only freedom in your mind, but also freedom from wrongdoing in your country, so that El Salvador can come alive and be a happy place again.

'I tell you that Jesus is before us this very moment saying, "I will heal you; be clean." If you receive the cleansing that He offers, you will be free from all that is holding you captive at this moment. You are going to bring about the liberty of your country starting in your own heart. You can be free right now if you accept Jesus Christ into your heart.'

I then told them that if they wanted this real freedom I wanted to pray with them. One by one, young people stood up until more than half of the group were on their feet.

After they had accepted Christ, the three of us, along with the young pastor, went and prayed for each of them individually.

One of the youths, who had confessed to having been a guerrilla, told me he felt free for the first time in his life. 'I'm now going to fight only for Jesus. I'm going to become a guerrilla for Christ.' It was an emotional moment.

Next day, Adalid had to leave to attend to urgent business in another country. In the meantime Dan and I were given a tour, by a Christian leader, of the bombed-out buildings that scar the city. Later we visited a pastor at a large San Salvador church.

'How are the Christians faring in all the troubles?' I asked him.

He looked grave. 'In the rural areas there have been many killings. Often evangelical believers are looked upon with suspicion by both the right and the left because they will not take up a political stance –'

'So they get shot by both sides,' I interjected.

'That can be the case,' he nodded.

'But,' I asked, 'what about in the cities?'

'Some weeks ago, the eldest son of a family in our church was accused of being a terrorist. When the National Guard gets information like this, they don't take someone in for questioning, they just go in with their guns blazing.

'They knocked on the door of this particular home, and when the boy answered the door they chased him into the house. The mother and her daughter tried to protect him, but they just blasted away and killed all three of them. That sort of thing is happening in our country all the time these days.'

Even as we spoke, an explosion went off in the distance, then another, until four bombs had exploded in a thirty-minute period. And later that evening, a blast shook our very hotel, shattering all the windows down one side. We joined the scores of people rushing out to see what had happened.

As I surveyed the scene, I saw a group of well-dressed young men discussing something urgently. Then one of them approached my companion.

'Are you a journalist?' he asked Dan in English.

Dan nodded and explained that he was from England.

'Would you like to know why we planted the bomb?'

Dan nodded again, not quite knowing how to react.

'This attorney had been on television earlier this afternoon, criticising the terrorists. We decided to teach him a lesson and so we left a package for him on his doorstep.'

Dan was dumbstruck.

'Would you like a tour of the area where we have planted bombs in the last few days? I'd feel honoured to show you around.'

The young terrorist spoke very good English. I remembered those earnest young people who the previous day had handed their lives over to Christ. Yet here was another prepared to kill and to impose his will on others. He was out in the open wanting to use a journalist in his group's propaganda campaign.

I desperately tried to catch Dan's eye and warn him to get out of the situation as quickly as possible. Fortunately, he did see me, made his excuses and managed to leave.

We went back to our room and began to pray for this young man and for all the young people of this tragic land, that there would be a real revival of God's love and that they would look for solutions other than those of the bomb and the bullet.

Next morning, we found the same taxi driver who had dropped us off in the *barrio*. He had agreed to take us by a roundabout route to the airport, explaining that taxis were ambushed daily.

As he drove, the cabbie told us that he was planning to flee the country the next day to Guatemala.

'My friend,' I told him, as we finally entered the airport, 'wherever you run to it will be dangerous. All over the world there are troubles. It will only be safe for those who are believers when God sets up His Kingdom through Jesus Christ.'

He smiled in a far-off way. 'I wish I could be part of that Kingdom . . .'

'You can,' I said earnestly. 'You really can.'

24. Which Liberation?

The tropical rains beat down on the mountain hideaway where some eighty Christian leaders from all over Central America had converged for one of our Open Doors 'Survival and Victory' seminars.

Because of the blanket of water that was dropping out of the angry sky, it was hard to see San José, the capital city of Costa Rica, stretching away in the distance below our site.

I stood under the shelter of the porch with Adalid. He had now really caught the vision of what we were endeavouring to do in Latin America. Adalid had helped to organise this seminar and had also supervised the complicated travel arrangements for the delegates, many of whom were from revolutionary situations in Central America.

He turned and pointed to some of the men who were sitting quietly waiting for the seminar to begin.

'Peter, do you know that many of these pastors here have been accused of being counter-revolutionaries? Some have even been threatened.'

One pastor told me of his own particular experience.

'I was recently holding a crusade in my area at which many were coming to know Christ. Suddenly, armed soldiers burst in and stopped the meeting. They smashed up all our equipment and attacked some of the congregation. They ordered me to hold no more meetings. No other explanation was given. I still don't know what I had done wrong.'

Adolfo, another pastor, chipped in: 'I have received

several anonymous letters saying that if I don't stop preaching the Gospel and instead start speaking out in favour of the revolution, I will be killed.

'I must confess to you, my brother, that at first I was very frightened. I asked the Lord what I should do. Then I came to this passage.'

He fluttered the pages of his Bible until he came to John 10:11, 12 and 13 . . . the good shepherd lays down his life for the sheep. He who is a hireling and not a shepherd, whose own the sheep are not, sees the wolf coming and leaves the sheep and flees; and the wolf snatches them and scatters them.'

Adolfo paused briefly.

'Don't you see, Peter? "He flees because he is a hireling and cares nothing for the sheep." I had to decide which kind of shepherd I was. If being a pastor was only a job for me, I should definitely flee for my life. But if God had called me to do this job, I had to be ready to lay down my life.'

I admired his decision, for I knew full well that one day his life might be required of him.

Soon the seminar was underway. I stood as I watched the slides entitled, 'Marx, Lenin, Mao and Christ,' which demonstrate that Communism is actually a religion and how this atheist philosophy, so opposed to Christianity, actually uses religious symbolism to put over its revolutionary theories.

I was delighted to see that my younger brother, Ricardo, was in the audience. He had slipped in just after we had started. Ricardo was now a student at the seminary where Olivia was a professor, and where Cesar had almost caused that strike.

When a break in proceedings came, I pulled Ricardo aside and held him tight.

'My young brother, it is so good to see you again. It must be a year since I was last with you. How is your wife, Elizabeth, and your two daughters?'

'Oh, they are fine, Peter, but we all miss Mexico.'

As the interval was short, I went on urgently. 'Ricardo, I

want to ask you a question that is worrying me very much. I have noticed that words like "liberation", "injustice", and "revolution" are being used very often by Christians today. How, for instance, is the word "liberation" understood in your seminary?'

Ricardo paused to gather his thoughts.

'Peter, you will probably know that much of this so-called "liberation theology" stems from Luke 4:18 which says: "The spirit of the Lord is upon me, because he has anointed me to preach good news to the poor. He has sent me to proclaim release to the captives, and recovering of sight to the blind, to set at liberty those who are oppressed, to proclaim the acceptable year of the Lord."

'Jesus came, I believe,' he went on, choosing his words carefully, 'to liberate us from original sin, and from the chains of bondage to a set of rules. Liberty was to be restored in man, also the right to be called His sons, so that this can orientate us towards the needs of man, illuminated by faith and guided by the Holy Spirit.

'I believe many people today abuse the term "liberty", translating it into injustice, and sometimes violence.'

I smiled at his complicated words.

'Ricardo, I think I can understand what you are saying, but must you use that hard-to-follow jargon of the seminary? We all have to learn to speak the language of the people.'

He chuckled. 'Peter, if you think my words are complicated, you should read some of Olivia's books. By the way, have you seen any of them?'

I shook my head, and Ricardo suggested that he bring some to my hotel later so we could look at them together.

When we met later on, Ricardo spread out a selection of Olivia's books on the table in the coffee shop.

His face was alight with pride.

'You know, we have a brilliant sister. She has raised, in these publications, many important topics about the unfairness of Latin American Society. And she has some interesting things to say to the Church about liberation. Everything she writes is based on the Bible, but her interpretation of Scripture is a little controversial.'

We had had our cups filled with steaming coffee, and Ricardo began reading from *The Hour for Life* (*Aportes-Dei*): ' "It is evident that the faith has been used to legitimise the status quo. Everyone knows that the Gospel preaches life. Jesus said: 'I have come so you may have life, and have it in abundance,' but in Latin America what we experience is poverty and misery: death. Where is that life?" '

He paused there.

'You know, Peter,' he said earnestly, 'in the past, we Christians have given little or no attention to the Biblical passages that speak of the suffering of the people of God through oppression and poverty. Today, though, many are going to the opposite extreme, and using the passages to justify even violence. They've misunderstood the proper biblical context.'

I agreed wholeheartedly. ' "Abundant life", as Olivia is pointing out, comes from following Jesus. "A man's life does not consist in the abundance of his possessions",' I quoted from Luke 12:15.

Ricardo nodded and turned back to Olivia's thought-provoking book.

' "It is also known that the Gospel preaches love: 'He that does not love his brother does not know God.' Nevertheless what we sense all around us is oppression and exploitation. Where is that love?" '

Ricardo looked up, as if seeking a response from me.

'Ricardo, I think the measure that God lives in a life is the measure that that person can give love to others. Because God is love. If we do not have love in our hearts, we cannot give love to others.'

Ricardo stopped me there. 'You know as well, my brother, oppressions and exploitation are not new things,' he told me. 'Biblical history shows this beyond a doubt.'

He then surprised me with his knowledge of the Old Testament.

'There are two main terms in Hebrew that designate oppression and the resultant poverty. One is *anah*, which

183

appears 85 times in the Old Testament to designate the degradation of the human being, the imposition of power and the sexual violation of women. The other is *asaq*, and this appears some 61 times in the Old Testament, to show the violent spoiling of something and therefore the impoverishment of a person.

'And I could go on from the New Testment, although terms referring to oppression and poverty are much less frequent there.'

By now he had become very excited. He smiled broadly when he realised how his fervour had attracted attention from others in the coffee shop.

'Now listen to this next bit in Olivia's book,' he told me in a lower voice.

' "The Gospel preaches liberty: 'The truth shall make you free.' What we find among our peoples is repression. Where is that liberty? Where is the life, the love and the liberty preached by the Gospel? Obviously something has happened in our reading of the Word of God. What originally should have meant *struggle*, *life*, *liberation*, has been replaced with *passivity*, *resignation*, *submission*. In other words, the Gospel has been reduced to individualistic and spiritualistic terms." '

I felt my face flush.

'But, Ricardo, the same passage in John 8:36 says, "So if the Son makes you free, you will be free indeed." Surely, what the Bible is talking about here is the liberty from sin. When that has been handled, then people are able to handle the other liberty. Sin is really the worst oppressor of our lives. But when we come to know Christ and He makes us free, we don't want to be unjust to others any more. We want to treat them properly. 'The problem of the human heart has to be dealt with first. Then there will be real liberty and justice in the world.'

I could see Ricardo agreed with what I was saying. He looked down at Olivia's book and shook his head.

'It seems to me, Peter, that we and Olivia have a different interpretation of the Bible.'

I hesitated for a moment.

'I don't know if it is exactly that. Maybe we see the struggle of the people in Latin America from different points of view. So we place a different emphasis on the practical and moral outworkings of Scripture. But as you can see, our intentions are not selfish. We all want the best for the people; it's just that we find different methods for bringing that about.'

I pointed out that all of our family, Nellie, Olivia, Cesar, Ruben and even Ricardo himself had a burden for Latin America. But we were all helping the people in different ways.

Ricardo turned back to Olivia's book. 'Now Peter, I want your honest reaction to this: "The hour for Latin America is to struggle (fight for) the reconquest of life for the popular majorities (masses). The struggle has to be constant and permanent." '

I thought for a moment.

'My dear brother, I don't know which one of us is right, but I can say that all of us have committed our lives for the good of the people on this continent.'

I opened my Bible again, this time to II Chronicles 7:14, and read the well-known verse, ' "If my people who are called by my name humble themselves, and pray and seek my face, and turn from their wicked ways, then I will hear from heaven, and will forgive their sin and heal their land." '

'This means that we, the believers of Latin America, can make a big difference. We can start by transforming our words into actions. We should be feeding the poor, being a force for justice, taking care of the elderly. As Brother Andrew says, "All these revolutions are taking place because the Church in the past didn't pay its invoices to the poor and downtrodden when it should have done so."

'I recognise that the Church has been hiding itself behind four walls. It has been spiritualising the Bible and forgetting the world outside. So I agree with Olivia that this is the time in Latin America when the Church has to change its attitude. Otherwise it will be too late. The devil will bring all his evil forces to confuse and take over this continent completely.'

I paused, 'Ricardo, I can tell you that if that happens, *real slavery* will take place. People will then not even have the liberty to think.'

I knew I had to go on preaching the message of Christ as long as I had breath. His was the only liberation for Latin America.

Epilogue: Pillow Talk

The happy chatter of Christmas pervaded the room. For the first time in ten years our whole family was back together again in our parents' Mexico City home. We had been released by our own husbands and wives for this special reunion.

The women of the family had followed the usual Mexican tradition of serving a meal of hot tamales, made deliciously spicy with various hot sauces, followed by succulent pieces of turkey. We had all spilled drops of sauce on our Sunday-best clothes, but no one cared.

After the food, we all sat around the large table sipping our mugs of hot chocolate. It was then that I, as the eldest brother, brought the gathering to order.

'Hey, now, everyone be quiet. I want Mama to make a speech.'

The conversation hushed to silence as she rose unsteadily to her feet.

'My little children . . .' Her lower lip quivered with emotion. 'I can't believe we are all together again. It is like the old days again. But now you have all grown so big, so clever.'

Those deep dark eyes looked into mine and held their gaze.

'Hey, Mama, we haven't grown up. We all feel young in our hearts,' was all I could stammer out.

'What are you talking about, Peter?' chuckled Cesar, his eyes twinkling as he spoke. 'You look as if you will soon be needing a walking stick.'

'Hey Cesar, I'll thump –'

'Children, children.' Papa clapped his hands, taking over the responsibility for restoring order.

Mama's tone was now deadly serious. 'My children, I am worried for all of you. I believe that your lives could be in great danger.' She turned to Cesar. 'You, my son: your work for the revolution could cause you many problems. And you, Ruben, you once told me how you were nearly killed by the peasants you were trying to help in the villages.'

She then looked back at me with those big eyes.

'Peter, you are probably in the most danger because you are moving against the current in Latin America. You are making a stand against things that you feel are wrong.'

Mama systematically went through the dangers each member of the family faced, then added: 'I pray every night that we can be together again for good, not just for one occasion like this.'

Then her face creased into a smile.

'My children, I want to let you into a secret that I have never told you before.'

She paused for a moment, and then launched into her confession. 'I was once a revolutionary, myself. When I was a young teacher, before Papa and I were married, I once marched with the Socialists here in Mexico. We were demonstrating for change.'

She looked at me over her glasses.

'Peter,' she continued, 'I'll be honest with you. I didn't really know what it meant to be a Socialist. We poor people in those days were told to be Socialists, so we were. They gave us banners and told us to march. We wanted change – there was so much wrong then, as now. And I suppose my mother worried about me, as I do about all of you. It's a mother's right to worry. But I know that it is more important to accept God's will in this. Whatever He wants for your lives, I will accept.'

As she sat down, we all applauded her, and I went over and kissed her. The others followed.

'Do you think we could ever all work together?' Papa suggested.

'I think that we should start a co-operative,' said Ruben. 'We could all pool our talents and produce something really worthwhile for Latin America.'

'Like what?' Ricardo asked.

'How about a publishing company? I could be the main editor,' Olivia chipped in.

'But you would want to write everything, my sister,' I retorted. 'I think we should help the people of Latin America with a chain of Fixed Price Stores. Then they could buy cheaply the essentials of life.'

'I think that's a crazy idea,' objected Rosa. 'What do you know about running a shop, Peter?'

'No,' chimed Papa, 'I think that's good. I could be the security man. And you, Maria, you could be the medical adviser.'

'No, I want to be the cashier. The person who adds up all the money,' she laughed.

As our crazy, but happy, conversation continued, Nellie stood up.

'Be quiet!' she ordered in a briskly professional voice. 'On behalf of the people of this community I feel insulted by what you men have said. I am going to make you suffer for your insults.'

'What are you talking about?'

I was silenced by Rosa, who by now had a provocative smile on her face. Her eyes were flashing.

'On behalf of the Women's Liberation Movement,' she said defiantly, 'I am also insulted, and I feel that there is only one solution to this situation.'

'What?' we chorused.

'This,' she yelled, as she produced a pillow from behind her back and swung it into my face. 'It must be a fight to the death. The men versus the women.' It was a revival of an old family custom for letting off steam.

With that we all piled into our parents' bedroom and armed ourselves with pillows. Feathers were soon flying all over the room.

For fully fifteen minutes, our 'war' was in full flight. Chairs were toppled over, some china was smashed. The

189

room was filled with laughter. Eyes were alive with fun. All our disagreements were forgotten.

Finally, Papa yelled for us to stop.

'You will wreck our flat,' he shouted, genuine concern in his voice.

As everyone calmed down, I turned to him. 'Papa, we have a present for you.' All the pillows flew through the air knocking him flat. He was soon helpless with laughter, tears of happiness coursing down his cheeks. Feathers gently floated downwards as we finally dusted ourselves off and rose to our feet.

'O.K., everyone,' I called, 'let's sit down. I've something I want to say to you all.'

Soon we were all seated. 'I think we all realise that it is a real blessing to be together at this time. All of us are serving the Lord in the way we believe is right.'

I looked over at Mama, who sat with her Bible cradled in her hands.

'Mama, we want you to know that you have directed us in the "royal way", and you can see here today that it has been a good road for us to walk.'

Papa squinted with pleasure as I raised my eyes to look at his weather-beaten face.

'Papa has also taught us that it is right to fight against adversity, not just to accept it. He has been almost blind for many years, yet he has not let that stop his work in providing for us. He has been a wonderful example to us all. I now want us all to acknowledge our love and respect for you both.'

With that we all stood and applauded heartily and then, as the eldest son, I went over and embraced them both. By now, in true Mexican fashion, the tears were flowing freely.

'I have a reading for this special occasion,' I continued, opening my Bible.

'I want us to remember that Jesus came at a time of revolution, of hunger and terrible trouble, and lived among the people of His day.

'The times then were in many ways like those we see today in Latin America. But He specially chose to come at that traumatic time. He didn't shy away from troubles. He faced them, and identified with the suffering people of His day.'

I turned to Philippians 2:5–11 and read aloud.

' "Have this mind among yourselves, which you have in Christ Jesus, who, though he was in the form of God, did not count equality with God a thing to be grasped, but emptied himself, taking the form of a servant, being born in the likeness of men. And being found in human form he humbled himself and became obedient unto death, even death on a cross. Therefore God has highly exalted him and bestowed on him the name which is above every name, that at the name of Jesus every knee should bow, in heaven and on earth and under the earth, and every tongue confess that Jesus Christ is Lord, to the glory of God the Father." '

The passage excited me, as it always did. 'This message has to be proclaimed all over Latin America,' I emphasised to my family.

'By the Grace of God, we were chosen to spread this message, not because we were worthy, but because God in His mercy is giving us that privilege. The prophets in the Bible didn't ask to be prophets. They were just chosen by God. I think that in the same way, we were called and placed in a situation we didn't ask for. But it is thrilling to be able to share this life-changing message.

'We are prophets in a continent full of violent revolution. Let's be faithful to our calling. It doesn't matter what adversities we face; let's get on with the task the best way we can. I believe one of our responsibilities as a family is to announce the justice of God. We also have to serve the people in their physical needs. But most important of all, we need to preach the imminent coming of the Lord to establish His eternal kingdom, where there will no longer be injustice, sorrow and hunger. We can tell people of a place where there will only be peace, liberty and happiness.'

There was a moment of silence as heads nodded with understanding. Then I turned to Rosa and asked her to get out her guitar.

'Let's sing some carols,' I said.

We began singing, 'Silent night, holy night'. Our family choir filled the room with beautiful music.

Suddenly, Mama stood up and held up her hand.

'Before we sing again, I want to say something.' She looked tenderly at us all. 'My children, you have proved one thing today. You have proved that although you disagree on many things, you can still love each other. Love is the only answer for our continent which is in such turmoil. And that love comes only from God.

'You have proved today, my family, that love has conquered for all of you – my "Prophets of Revolution".'

More information concerning Peter Gonzales' ministry and that of Open Doors with Brother Andrew can be obtained from the following addresses:

P.O. Box 47
3850 AA Ermelo,
Holland

P.O. Box 6
Standlake, Witney
Oxon, OX8 7SP
England

P.O. Box 2250
Orange, CA 92669
USA